# SAVING ENDANGERED SPECIES

# THE
# SNOW LEOPARD
## Help Save This Endangered Species!

# Glenn Scherer and
# Marty Fletcher

MyReportLinks.com Books

an imprint of

 **Enslow Publishers, Inc.**

Box 398, 40 Industrial Road
Berkeley Heights, NJ 07922
USA

MyReportLinks.com Books, an imprint of Enslow Publishers, Inc. MyReportLinks®
is a registered trademark of Enslow Publishers, Inc.

**Library of Congress Cataloging-in- Publication Data**

Scherer, Glenn.
  The snow leopard : help save this endangered species! / Glenn Scherer and Marty Fletcher.
    p. cm. — (Saving endangered species)
  Includes bibliographical references and index.
  ISBN-13: 978-1-59845-040-8
  ISBN-10: 1-59845-040-9
1. Snow leopard—Juvenile literature. I. Fletcher, Marty. II. Title.
  QL737.C23S33 2007
  599.75'55—dc22

                                        2006023506

Printed in the United States of America

10 9 8 7 6 5 4 3 2 1

**To Our Readers:**
Through the purchase of this book, you and your library gain access to the Report Links that specifically
back up this book.
The Publisher will provide access to the Report Links that back up this book and will keep these Report
Links up to date on **www.myreportlinks.com** for five years from the book's first publication date.
We have done our best to make sure all Internet addresses in this book were active and appropriate when
we went to press. However, the author and the Publisher have no control over, and assume no liability
for, the material available on those Internet sites or on other Web sites they may link to.
The usage of the MyReportLinks.com Books Web site is subject to the terms and conditions stated on the
Usage Policy Statement on **www.myreportlinks.com**.
A password may be required to access the Report Links that back up this book. The password is found
on the bottom of page 4 of this book.
Any comments or suggestions can be sent by e-mail to comments@myreportlinks.com or to the address
on the back cover.

**Photo Credits:** © Corel Corporation, pp. 16–17, 23, 52–53, 60, 73, 85, 95, 108–109, 113;
© Falk Kienas/Shutterstock.com, p. 70; © Glen Gaffney/Shutterstock.com, p. 1; © Pichugin
Dmitry/Shutterstock.com, p. 39; ARKive, p. 87; BBC News, p. 40; Big Cat Rescue, p. 110; CNN.com,
p. 47; Defenders of Wildlife, p. 62; Enslow Publishers, Inc., p. 5; International Snow Leopard Trust,
p. 91; International Society for Endangered Cats, p. 97; IUCN-World Conservation Union, p. 76;
MyReportLinks.com Books, p. 4; National Public Radio, p. 45; NationalGeographic.com, pp. 13, 54; PBS,
p. 65; Philadelphia Zoo, p. 19; Photo courtesy of Snow Leopard Trust, p. 37; Photos.com, pp. 3, 10–11,
26, 29, 34–35, 80, 82; Radio Free Europe/Radio Liberty, p. 43; Shutterstock.com, pp. 48–49; Snow
Leopard Conservancy, p. 93; The International Fund for Animal Welfare, p. 107; *The Seattle Times,* p. 66;
The Snow Leopard Network, p. 99; The University of Michigan Museum of Zoology, p. 30;
TheBigCats.com, p. 58; TRAFFIC, pp. 68, 100; U.S. Department of State, p. 89; U.S. Fish and Wildlife
Service, pp. 21, 115; U.S. House of Representatives, p. 104; Wildlife Conservation Network, p. 15;
Wildlife Conservation Society, p. 75; Woodland Park Zoo, p. 33; World Wildlife Fund, pp. 79, 102.

**Cover Photo:** © Glen Gaffney/Shutterstock.com.

# CONTENTS

# MyReportLinks.com Books
## Great Books, Great Links, Great for Research!

**T**he Internet sites featured in this book can save you hours of research time. These Internet sites—we call them **"Report Links"**—are constantly changing, but we keep them up to date on our Web site.

When you see this "Approved Web Site" logo, you will know that we are directing you to a great Internet site that will help you with your research.

Give it a try! Type **http://www.myreportlinks.com** into your browser, click on the series title and enter the password, then click on the book title, and scroll down to the Report Links listed for this book.

The Report Links will bring you to great source documents, photographs, and illustrations. MyReportLinks.com Books save you time, feature Report Links that are kept up to date, and make report writing easier than ever! A complete listing of the Report Links can be found on pages 116–117 at the back of the book.

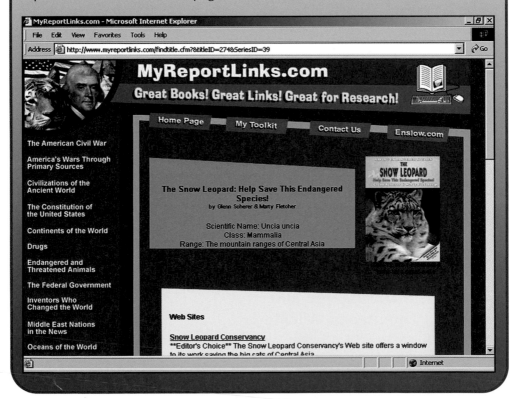

Please see "To Our Readers" on the copyright page for important information about this book, the MyReportLinks.com Web site, and the Report Links that back up this book.

## Please enter **SLS1678** if asked for a password.

# Snow Leopard
## Range Map

RUSSIA

KAZAKHSTAN

MONGOLIA

UZBEKISTAN

KYRGYZSTAN

TURKMENISTAN

TAJIKISTAN

CHINA

IRAN

AFGHANISTAN

KASHMIR

PAKISTAN

NEPAL

BHUTAN

INDIA

BANGLADESH

Gulf of Oman

MYANMAR
(BURMA)

LAOS

VIETNAM

ARABIAN SEA

Bay
of
Bengal

THAILAND

SOUTH
CHINA
SEA

CAMBODIA

INDIA

ANDAMAN
SEA

Gulf of
Thailand

INDIA

SRI LANKA

INDIA

MALAYSIA

BRUNEI

= **Areas where snow leopards
may be found**

N

# Snow Leopard Facts

▶ **Scientific Name**
*Uncia uncia*

▶ **Size and Weight**
The head and body length of the average adult snow leopard is 39 to 51 inches (99 to 130 centimeters), with the tail length nearly as long as the animal's body. The weight range is 99 to 121 pounds (45 to 55 kilograms) for males, and 77 to 88 pounds (35 to 40 kilograms) for typically smaller females.

▶ **Current Range**
Tall mountain ranges in Central Asia. The usable range of the snow leopard is over 1,000,000 square miles (2,590,000 square kilometers), half of which is in China. Its range encompasses seven major mountain ranges in the following twelve countries: Afghanistan, Bhutan, China, India, Mongolia, Nepal, Pakistan, Russia, Kazakhstan, Kyrgyzstan, Tajikistan, and Uzbekistan.

▶ **Habitat**
Snow leopards live in high treeless rocky tundra in summer and lower alpine meadows and rhododendron forests in winter. They are most at home on the steepest cliffs and highest open ridges, in the most rugged mountain country. They are also found in semiarid wild shrubland, grassland, or steppe vegetation in China, and sometimes visit coniferous forests. They usually live at altitudes from 9,800 feet to 14,800 feet (3,000 to 4,500 meters) above sea level.

▶ **Diet**
Mostly wild sheep and goats, including bharal, a Himalayan blue sheep that is actually gray in color; argali, another kind of wild sheep; and Asian ibex and markhor, types of wild goats. They eat pikas (also called rock rabbits), marmots (mountain rodents), hares, and game birds, especially chukar partridge and snowcocks. At lower altitudes, snow leopards will prey on gazelles, wild boars, red pandas, tragopan and monal pheasants, and other birds. When wild prey is not available, they also eat domestic livestock, causing conflict with herders. Recent studies have found that in certain areas of India, the snow leopards' diet includes a substantial amount of vegetation, unusual for carnivores.

▶ **Age at Sexual Maturity**
Two or three years

▶ **Number of Cubs per Litter**
There is almost no information about wild births, but in zoos, there are usually one to three cubs per litter.

## ▶ Gestation Period

Mating occurs between December and March throughout Central Asia. There is a 90- to 100-day gestation period. Cubs are born in April, May, and June.

## ▶ Size of Newborns

Again, the only information comes from zoos. Newborn snow leopards weigh between 0.7 to 1.56 pounds (318 to 708 grams) at birth. They have a daily average weight gain of approximately 0.1 pound (48 grams) per day.

## ▶ Life Span

In captivity, snow leopards have been known to live for twenty-one years. Life span in the wild is unknown but is thought to be significantly shorter.

## ▶ Status

The total world population of snow leopards remaining in the wild is estimated at between 4,000 to 7,000 animals. There are approximately 500 snow leopards in 150 zoos worldwide, with 236 of those animals in the United States. Experts stress that these estimates of wild populations have been based on limited and mostly out-of-date surveys, and with the cats moving across country boundaries, they are sometimes counted twice. In other areas, where wars have been fought or continue, there may be fewer snow leopards now than in the past. In places where their protections are upheld the best, their numbers may have grown. Researchers are now beginning to use new technologies, including camera traps, to make better estimates of the snow leopard population.

## ▶ Major Threats

Habitat loss, habitat fragmentation and degradation, lack of wild prey, retaliation for killing livestock, and hunting and poaching for pelts used in clothing and for bones and body parts used in traditional Chinese medicine.

*The mountains gave man soil, provided him with food, and stored his water, but he has taken almost everything, leaving the earth's bones bare. The snow leopard might well serve as symbol of man's commitment to the future of the mountain world.*

—George B. Schaller,
*Stones of Silence: Journeys in the Himalaya*

# Chapter 1

# TRACKING—AND SAVING—AN ELUSIVE CAT

**High** in the Himalayas, a mountain range in Central Asia that is home to the world's highest peaks, in one of the coldest, harshest environments on Earth, lives a great cat. It is an animal that few people outside its habitat had even seen thirty years ago, and it remains an elusive creature to the researchers trying to track and study it today.

Still, one scientist's glimpse of a snow leopard, while actually studying the cat's favored prey, convinced him and later others that the world needed to learn more about this mysterious animal. In 1970, Dr. George B. Schaller, considered by many to be the most important field biologist of our time, was in northern Pakistan. He had traveled to one of the most remote and mountainous parts of the planet to study the life cycle of the bharal, the Himalyan blue sheep. What Schaller was rewarded with seeing was the sheep's predator: a snow leopard. Schaller was able to observe the cat and its cub for a week. Only the second Westerner to actually see the species in its native habitat, he became the first to photograph it there. The

Researchers believe there are fewer than seven thousand snow leopards remaining in the wild. These elusive big cats of the mountains of Central Asia are threatened most of all by human activities.

publication of his photograph in *National Geographic* magazine brought the elusive animal to the world's attention. Schaller writes dramatically of one of his first meetings with the snow leopard in Pakistan's Chitral Valley.

> Hunched against December's cold, I scanned the slope, looking for the snow leopard which was somewhere a thousand feet above near a goat it had killed the previous day. . . . Slowly I climbed upward, kicking steps into the snow and angling toward a spur of rock from which to survey the valley. Soon scree [loose rock debris at the base of a cliff] gave way to a chaos of boulders and rocky outcrops, the slopes motionless and silent as if devoid of life.
>
> Then I saw the snow leopard, a hundred and fifty feet away, peering at me from the spur, her body so well molded into the contours of the boulders that she seemed a part of them. Her smoky-gray coat sprinkled with black rosettes perfectly complemented the rocks and snowy wastes, and her pale eyes conveyed an image of immense solitude. As we watched each other the clouds descended once more entombing us and bringing more snow. Perhaps sensing that I meant her no harm, she sat up. Though snow soon capped her head and shoulders, she remained, silent and still, seemingly impervious to the elements. Wisps of clouds swirled around, transforming her into a ghost creature, part myth and part reality. . . . Then the snow fell more thickly, and, dreamlike, the cat slipped away as if she had never been.[1]

Schaller returned to the Chitral Valley less than four years later, hoping to attach radio collars to the cats to track them and learn more about them, but nearly all of them were gone, either trapped or shot for their pelts. He would return again in the late 1980s to learn more about the snow leopard. Still, it was Schaller's first view of a snow leopard that inspired others, including the conservationist Dr. Rodney Jackson, founder of the Snow Leopard Conservancy. Jackson saw Schaller's photograph of snow leopards in *National Geographic* and decided he too wanted to see the elusive cat. In the early 1980s, Jackson and his partner, Darla Hillard, joined later by biologist Gary Ahlborn, embarked on a scientific study of the snow leopard. They traveled to the forbiddingly cold Himalayan high peaks

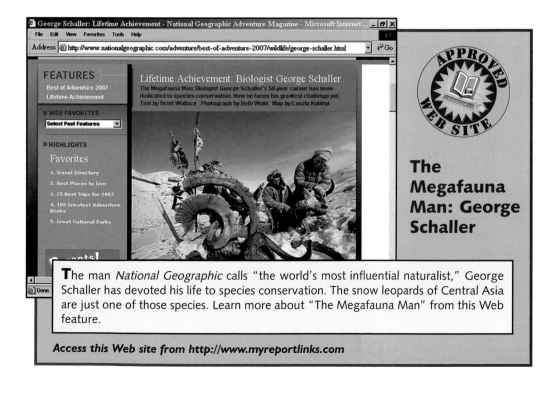

**The Megafauna Man: George Schaller**

The man *National Geographic* calls "the world's most influential naturalist," George Schaller has devoted his life to species conservation. The snow leopards of Central Asia are just one of those species. Learn more about "The Megafauna Man" from this Web feature.

*Access this Web site from http://www.myreportlinks.com*

of Nepal where they became the first to capture and radio-collar the cats, during a four-year study.

Jackson's studies of the snow leopard, along with those of other scientists, including Doctors Tom McCarthy and Charudutt Mishra of the International Snow Leopard Trust, have contributed a great deal of what we now know about the species. Their work has also helped to save the snow leopard from the brink of extinction. Today, the snow leopard is protected in every country in which it lives—even if those protections are not always as well enforced as they could be. Private, nonprofit organizations such as the International Snow Leopard Trust, founded in 1981 by Helen Freeman, and the Snow Leopard Conservancy, founded by Dr. Jackson, are actively engaged in the effort to save this animal. But ultimately, it will be the people who share the snow leopards' lands who will decide whether these beautiful cats survive.

## ▶Why Snow Leopards Matter

Why is it important to save snow leopards? Why should we, who live a world away from these creatures, care about what happens to them?

There are many reasons. First, if humans cause snow leopards to go extinct, we will be extinguishing a beautiful animal that has spent millions of years perfectly adapting itself to its unique habitat. Such a loss would be devastating to scientists

Snow leopard conservation, Himalaya, India, Nepal - Microsoft Internet Explorer

File   Edit   View   Favorites   Tools   Help

Address http://www.wildnet.org/snowleopard.htm

**WCN**
WILDLIFE CONSERVATION NETWORK

HOME   ABOUT WCN   PARTNERS   FELLOWS   EVENTS   NEWS   DONATE   CONTACT US

## CONSERVATION FELLOWS

**Snow Leopard Conservancy - Rodney Jackson**
www.snowleopardconservancy.org

Dr. Rodney Jackson, Director of the Snow Leopard Conservancy, is committed to saving the snow leopard *(Uncia uncia)*. He is the leading expert on snow leopards and their habitat and is the recipient of the 1981 Rolex Award for Enterprise, based on his four-year radio-tracking study of ...ards in Nepal. He has pioneered the standardization of snow ...king methods and was the first to radio collar a snow leopard ...e is a member of the IUCN/SSC Cat Specialist Group. ...ney is working in India, Nepal, and other Himalayan countries ...ow leopard with remote cameras - producing some of the ...f natural snow leopard behavior in the wild.

RODNEY JACKSON PUTTING A RADIO COLLAR ON A SNOW LEOPARD.

The strikingly beautiful snow leopard remains one of the most mysterious

**T**he Wildlife Conservation Network supports the work of conservationists from around the world. On the **Wildlife Conservation Network: Conservation Fellows** page, Dr. Rodney Jackson, founder of the Snow Leopard Conservancy, is profiled.

who want to learn more about snow leopards, their behaviors, and their evolution.

Snow leopards are also stunning creatures that inspire people with their fierce beauty, grace, and wildness. Their loss would make the world a less beautiful, less wild place in which to live. "Words cannot begin to portray what it feels like to be surrounded by the habitat and spirit of such a magnificent creature," writes snow leopard biologist Rodney Jackson, "from the almost eerie and dominating silence of winter to the roar of a passing

If the snow leopard is to survive, its mountain ecosystem must also be protected.

storm, the soft plaintive calls of the white-rumped snowfinch or whistle-like sound of the horned lark, the conspicuously raucous black-billed magpie (our camp sentinel), or the strong pungent odor of a rock freshly scented by a snow leopard that passed by in the early morning light."[2]

Ecologists recognize that every creature has its special place in an ecosystem. When a species goes extinct, its loss can drastically affect the way the ecosystem functions or even cause it to fail.

There is another good reason to save snow leopards. Researchers are alarmed at how quickly our mountain ecosystems are being degraded. Mining, logging, and other activities to suit the needs of a growing and more-industrialized population are having a profound effect on lands that were once undeveloped. In this century, the world's great mountain ranges could become nearly barren of wildlife. To protect endangered species like the snow leopard, we also must protect the mountain ecosystems in which they and humans live. It is the people who live among the snow leopards that are capable of becoming their best guardians and can improve their own lives if their governments and ours help.

## ▶ What You Can Do

There is a lot you can do to help endangered species like the snow leopard. The most important thing you can do is to become an advocate for these endangered animals. This requires first of all that you learn everything you can about the species.

One of the most dramatic ways to learn about the snow leopard is to actually see one. There are approximately 500 snow leopards in 150 zoos worldwide, with 236 of those animals found in the United States. That means that it is likely that there is a snow leopard in a major zoo near you. Many of these zoos offer informative exhibits and programs featuring endangered species, such as the snow leopard, programs in which you can often actively participate. The Philadelphia Zoo, for

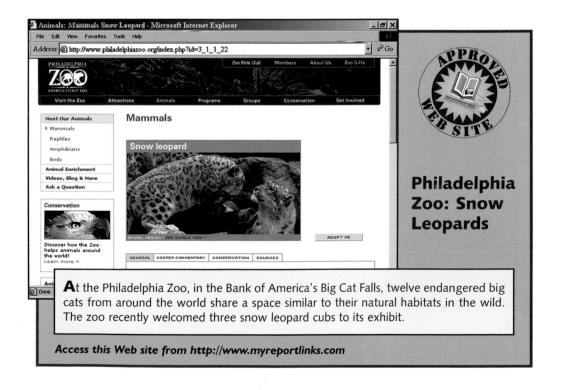

**Philadelphia Zoo: Snow Leopards**

**A**t the Philadelphia Zoo, in the Bank of America's Big Cat Falls, twelve endangered big cats from around the world share a space similar to their natural habitats in the wild. The zoo recently welcomed three snow leopard cubs to its exhibit.

*Access this Web site from http://www.myreportlinks.com*

example, has recently constructed the Bank of America Big Cat Falls, with "a stunning landscape of lush habitats and waterfalls where guests can come face to face with 12 endangered big cats from around the world [including snow leopards]."[3] When this area opened, it even featured three new playful snow leopard cubs. The exhibit not only allows you to watch the snow leopards' behaviors and their every movement, but it has also made an effort to house the cats in an environment as close as possible to their habitat in the wild. Each exhibit features plants similar to those found in the animals' home range. The snow leopards are also given rocky crags on which to play and rock dens in which to live. As the zoo's Web site describes it,

> At the center of the exhibit, a cascading 12-foot waterfall beckons kids to dash under its stream on their way to Base Camp, where families can pinball through an activity-filled research station. . . . Kids can take a cat personality test to find out which feline most closely matches their own personality and then watch as their own photo digitally morphs with the cat's face. They'll also get the chance to join the brand-new Zoo Kids Club and receive special e-newsletters, [and] exclusive invitations to Zoo events. . . . [4]

Other zoos around the country feature similar exhibits, including the Chattanooga Zoo in Tennessee, which got its first snow leopards in 2006. The snow leopards there are part of the

Nepalese Trading Post, an extension of the zoo's Himalayan Passage exhibit. "The exhibit is important to the zoo's mission of conservation and education because it shows how people in that region live with the animals of that region," says the zoo's executive director, Dardenelle Long.[5]

You can also learn more about snow leopards by visiting the Web sites of conservation organizations that have helped to save them, such as the Snow Leopard Conservancy, the International Snow Leopard Trust, the World Wildlife Fund, and the Wildlife Conservation Society. These sites not only help you become better educated about snow leopards, but some also invite you to "adopt" a

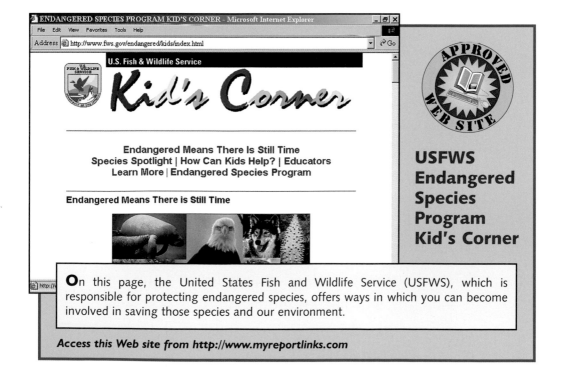

USFWS Endangered Species Program Kid's Corner

On this page, the United States Fish and Wildlife Service (USFWS), which is responsible for protecting endangered species, offers ways in which you can become involved in saving those species and our environment.

Access this Web site from http://www.myreportlinks.com

snow leopard by making a contribution to the organization.

With knowledge comes power. The more you know about an endangered species such as the snow leopard, the more you can communicate what you know to your friends and family. You can also organize letter-writing campaigns to the United Nations or the United States government seeking better protections for snow leopards. Ultimately, you may even want to grow up to become a wildlife biologist or conservation activist like George Schaller, Rodney Jackson, and others. The more you care, the better chance this endangered species has of surviving.

## ▶ What the Experts Say

The scientists involved in snow leopard conservation can also tell us why snow leopards should be saved. "For one thing, the snow leopard stands as a sensitive indicator or barometer of a healthy mountain environment," according to Rodney Jackson.[6] If snow leopards are thriving, then that means there are plenty of prey species such as bharal, or blue sheep, in the mountains, and that there is plenty of vegetation for those prey species to eat. With enough wild prey, the snow leopards will not kill domestic livestock, which means that the people who own that livestock will also thrive.

▲ *When a charismatic megaspecies such as the snow leopard is saved, all the other creatures in its ecosystem are also protected.*

"For another," says Jackson, "the snow leopard stands as a vital symbol of Asia's mountains—in scientific jargon, a 'charismatic megaspecies.' By protecting this species, home for others is assured."[7] A charismatic megaspecies (or mega-fauna) is a large endangered animal that attracts people's attention around the world and makes them want to pitch in to save it. Such animals include not only snow leopards, but most other big cats such as the Florida panther and Indian tiger as well as whales and gorillas. To save a charismatic megaspecies, the ecosystem in which it lives must also be saved. As a result all the lesser-known, less glamorous, species living in that habitat get saved as well. What is good for a charismatic megaspecies is good for the entire environment and all the creatures living in it. As Jackson concludes, "For those of us who have seen the wild snow leopard, there can be no other wish than this: Long may these exquisite creatures roam the cliffs and valleys, and long may they gaze across the wide, untrammeled vistas of their lofty mountain realm."[8]

**Chapter 2 ▶**

# ALL ABOUT
# SNOW LEOPARDS

**There** are thirty-six species of wild cats on Earth, including the snow leopard. Despite its name, the snow leopard is not thought to be closely related to the leopard or other members of the Pantherine group. Though once classified as part of the Pantherines, the snow leopard is now classified as the only member of the genus *Uncia*, giving it its scientific name: *Uncia uncia*. The word *uncia* is probably a corruption of the French word "once" or "lonce," which comes from the Latin *lynx,* a type of feline.[1]

The snow leopard is among the smallest of the world's big cats. One of the major differences between it and other big cats such as lions, tigers, and other leopards is its inability to roar. Unlike those species, the snow leopard has an underdeveloped tissue in its vocal chords that keeps it from letting out the kind of deep roar most people associate with big cats.[2]

## ▶ Perfectly Evolved for Its Environment and Its Prey

The snow leopard is ideally adapted to be a top predator in its snowy, high mountain environment.

▲ *Snow leopards are top predators in their food web, but their food in the wild has become more scarce because of the activities of humans.*

This endangered species is whitish-gray, tinged with yellow, and patterned with dark-gray rosettes (irregular rose-shaped open markings) and solid spots. This coloration allows it to blend in perfectly with the mountain landscape, whether that landscape consists of bare rocks in summer or deep snows in winter. Snow leopards molt, losing and regrowing their hair, twice a year, but the summer coat, while less dense, differs little in color or length from their winter one.

## ▶ Life at the Top

The snow leopard has other adaptations that allow it to live in the high mountain ranges of Central Asia. For example, it has an enlarged nasal cavity, so it can breathe more easily in the thin mountain air. It has shortened limbs to keep it low to the ground, helping it to be invisible in the stark landscape and to stay out of cold winds. Its adult shoulder height is only about 23.6 inches (60 centimeters), making it much shorter than the lions of lowland Africa or tigers of lowland Asia. The snow leopard has very well-developed chest muscles that enable it to climb and jump from one cliff to another.

The snow leopard is also adapted to deal with extreme temperature ranges, from temperatures above 80°F to −31°F (26° to −35°C). Its hair is dense, with woolly underfur that can grow as long as 4.7 inches (12 centimeters). Its tail is nearly as long as the entire rest of its body. That thick and bushy tail can be wrapped around the animal's body and face to provide extra warmth. The long tail also helps the snow leopard to balance itself as it springs from one rocky ledge to another.

The head and body length of the average adult snow leopard is 39 to 51 inches (99 to 129 centimeters), with the tail length an additional 31.5 to 39 inches (78 to 99 centimeters). The animals' weight range is 99 to 121 pounds (45 to 55 kilograms) for males, and 77 to 88 pounds (35 to 40 kilograms) for the typically smaller females. Its paws are very large and furry, functioning well as snowshoes and offering warmth and padding against sharp rocks.

The eyes of snow leopards are mounted in the front of their face, like those of humans, which gives the animals the good depth perception they need to judge distances to the prey species they are pouncing on. Their forepaws are equipped with long, retractable claws that can be used to grab and hold prey. Their rough tongue is designed to peel the skin of prey animals away from flesh, and flesh away from bone. Loose belly skin allows the big cat to be kicked by the goats and sheep they prey on with little chance of injury.

## ▶ Subspecies of Snow Leopards

Some scientists believe that there are several uniquely evolved subspecies of snow leopards.

*The tail of a snow leopard is nearly as long as the rest of its body, providing the big cat with needed warmth and stability.*

They point out that there are two major snow leopard ranges that do not actually touch each other, one in the Himalayas of Central Asia, and the other in Mongolia and Russia. They say that the animals could not possibly travel between these two regions to mate with each other, so they must be subspecies, but no one is really sure. There is good evidence that snow leopards can travel over 370 miles (600 kilometers) if they need to. Such travels would allow all the populations of snow leopards to potentially mingle at one time or another. Although snow leopards are listed

ADW: snowleopard.jpg - Microsoft Internet Explorer

File   Edit   View   Favorites   Tools   Help

Address http://animaldiversity.ummz.umich.edu/site/resources/david_blank/snowleopard.jpg/view_large.html

**A**nimal Diversity Web: *Uncia uncia*, a Web page from the University of Michigan Museum of Zoology's site, provides a comprehensive page of information about snow leopards and includes photographs of the species including this one, of a snow leopard in China's Urumqui Wildlife Park.

as a migratory species for conservation purposes, because they cross national boundaries, they are not migratory species in the sense that birds, whales, and other animals are.

The scientists who argue in favor of dividing the species into two subspecies of snow leopards list the Russian and Mongolian version of the animal as *Uncia uncia uncia*. They list the one in the Himalayas and China as *Uncia uncia uncioides*.

Other researchers think that there could be even more subspecies of snow leopard, caused by the isolation of one mountain range from another, preventing the animals from ever mating with each other. More genetic research will be needed to determine the answer to this question.

## ▶Efficient Predators

Snow leopards are opportunistic predators. As carnivores, or meat-eaters, they can kill prey up to three times their own weight, but they are also willing to feed on small mammals too. Acute senses of vision, hearing, and smell aid in hunting.

Their favorite foods are wild sheep and goats, including bharal (blue sheep that are actually gray in color), argali (another kind of wild sheep), and Asian ibex and markhor (types of wild goats). They also eat pikas, hares and game birds, especially chukar partridge and snowcocks. In China's Qinghai province, studies by George Schaller in the late 1980s found that 45 percent of a snow leopard's summer diet consisted of marmots. At lower altitudes, snow leopards will prey on gazelles, wild boars, red pandas, brilliantly colored tragopan and monal pheasants, and other birds. In captivity, their diet may be even more varied. At the Woodland Park Zoo in Seattle, snow leopards are fed a diet of commercially prepared feline food that includes the following: "mutton, beef knuckle bone, chicken, rabbits, beef heart, beef kidney, horse meat, ground turkey and chicks."[3]

## Not Just Meat-Eaters

Recent research has found, however, that these carnivores also eat vegetation. In a study in 2006, two biologists investigated conflicts between people and snow leopards in two areas of northern India's Spiti region where the cats were known to kill livestock. In one part of their study, they examined the scat, or fecal remains, of the snow leopards. They found that vegetation was often part of the snow leopard scat they examined, especially in the colder months when prey was unavailable.[4]

## Stalking Its Prey

In the wild, the snow leopard usually stalks its prey, then can spring up to 50 feet (15.25 meters) horizontally and 20 feet (6 meters) vertically to

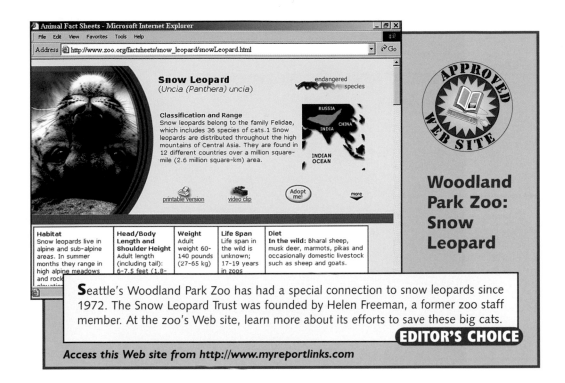

Animal Fact Sheets - Microsoft Internet Explorer

File Edit View Favorites Tools Help

Address http://www.zoo.org/factsheets/snow_leopard/snowLeopard.html Go

### Snow Leopard
(Uncia (Panthera) uncia)

endangered species

#### Classification and Range
Snow leopards belong to the family Felidae, which includes 36 species of cats.1 Snow leopards are distributed throughout the high mountains of Central Asia. They are found in 12 different countries over a million square-mile (2.6 million square-km) area.

RUSSIA

CHINA

INDIA

INDIAN OCEAN

printable version    video clip    Adopt me!    more

| Habitat | Head/Body Length and Shoulder Height | Weight | Life Span | Diet |
|---|---|---|---|---|
| Snow leopards live in alpine and sub-alpine areas. In summer months they range in high alpine meadows and rock | Adult length (including tail): 6-7.5 feet (1.8- | Adult weight 60-140 pounds (27-65 kg) | Life span in the wild is unknown; 17-19 years in zoos | In the wild: Bharal sheep, musk deer, marmots, pikas and occasionally domestic livestock such as sheep and goats. |

**S**eattle's Woodland Park Zoo has had a special connection to snow leopards since 1972. The Snow Leopard Trust was founded by Helen Freeman, a former zoo staff member. At the zoo's Web site, learn more about its efforts to save these big cats.

**EDITOR'S CHOICE**

*Access this Web site from http://www.myreportlinks.com*

**Woodland Park Zoo: Snow Leopard**

APPROVED WEB SITE

make a kill. But these cats are not really built for running, so they need to get very close to their prey before making a final lunge at it. While they are able to make huge leaps, it is probably rare that they do so, since the chances of them missing, if not flying off cliffs, is just too great.

In *Stones of Silence: Journeys in the Himalaya*, George Schaller describes the awesome fierce beauty of watching a snow leopard make a kill: The female snow leopard crouches, hidden in rocks and by its own camouflage for forty-five minutes, closely watching the goat. Then the snow leopard edges its way forward, body pressed tightly to the ground, edging one paw forward at a

Crouching on a rock ledge, this snow leopard is camouflaged from prey.

time until it reaches a boulder jutting out just above the goat. The big cat hunches, hesitates, and then leaps. It strikes the ground just behind the goat. The scared goat whirls about and tries to protect itself with its horns. The snow leopard rears back and avoids the blow from the sharp horns. The goat turns to flee and the snow leopard, much like a domestic cat jumping on a ball of yarn, pounces with its claws extended. Like a champion athlete, it gracefully leaps through the air and sinks its teeth into the throat of the running goat. The big cat also plunges its massive forepaws into the goat's shoulder. The chase is at an end. The goat sinks slowly to its knees and topples to its side. The snow leopard now patiently waits until the goat is dead before it devours its kill.[5]

## ▶ After the Kill

It is estimated that an adult snow leopard needs to prey on from twenty to thirty adult bharal every year to survive. In a study of radio-collared animals, it was found that adult snow leopards killed a large prey animal every ten to fifteen days. They remain with each large kill for up to three or four days, sometimes as much as a week, feeding on it daily. They must closely guard their kill against griffons (large vultures), crows, magpies, and other scavengers that would take the meat.

Biologists have been able to find snow leopard kills simply by looking for circling scavenger birds.

## Snow Leopards, Domestic Livestock, and People

The decline in wild sheep and goat populations, which can be tied in most areas to a rise in the number of livestock, has resulted in the snow leopard relying more and more on domestic livestock

▲ *Mongolian children cradle their goats. A decline in wild goats and sheep, both prey that the snow leopard feeds on, can be linked directly to an increase in domestic livestock in the big cats' range.*

for food. Domesticated animals are much easier for the big cat to kill on the open range because they do not have the strong instincts of wild animals anymore. When snow leopards kill livestock on the open range, however, the cats will typically kill only one animal while the others run away.

There are also many instances on record of snow leopards entering livestock sheds at night and killing goats and sheep inside. This happens because once a leopard gets inside a pen, the livestock panic and run, and their running triggers the cat's kill instinct until there is no more movement. When a family loses fifty or sixty animals to such attacks, it is a devastating loss. On the Tibetan Plateau, livestock losses average about 2 percent of all domestic livestock per village, but the percentage is greater, nearly 10 percent, in some other areas.

## ▶ Not Aggressive Toward Humans

Snow leopards are not seen as a threat to human beings by most scientists. A 1960s report by Russian biologists actually described the big cat's "playfulness and trusting nature."[6] There are only two reports of snow leopard attacks on people. One attack happened in the Soviet Union in 1940 when a snow leopard jumped two people. It was later found to be rabid, which explains the reason for the attack. Another attack is said to have

▲ A Himalayan village in Nepal. If people and snow leopards cannot learn to coexist peacefully, the big cats' future is a dismal one.

occurred on a Swedish hiker in Nepal during the 1970s. But almost always, snow leopards prefer to stay away from humans. Snow leopards are solitary cats, and crepuscular, which means that they are generally most active around dawn and dusk. But they are also known to have adapted their activity levels at different times to avoid people.

## ▶ Snow Leopard Habitat

The snow leopard habitat varies from high treeless rocky tundra in summer to lower alpine meadows and rhododendron forests in winter. They are most at home on the steepest cliffs and highest open ridges of the most rugged mountainous terrain. They are also found in semiarid wild

APPROVED WEB SITE

BBC News: "Snow Leopard Diary"

BBC NEWS | Technology | Snow Leopard Diary - Microsoft Internet Explorer

File   Edit   View   Favorites   Tools   Help

Address http://news.bbc.co.uk/1/hi/technology/6159767.stm   Go

BBC NEWS

▶ WATCH The News in 2 minutes

News services
Your news when you want it

News Front Page
World
UK
England
Northern Ireland
Scotland
Wales
Business
Politics
Health
Education
Science/Nature
Technology
Entertainment
Video and Audio
Have Your Say
Magazine
In Pictures
Country Profiles
Special Reports

Last Updated: Friday, 19 January 2007, 08:54 GMT

E-mail this to a friend      Printable version

**Snow Leopard Diary**

A research project is under way to learn more about the elusive snow leopard.

A team has travelled to the Chitral Gol National Park in the Pakistan-Afghanistan borders to attach Global Positioning Satellite (GPS) collars to five of the cats, to understand more about the animals' movements.

The team has already managed to fit a collar to one cat

With one snow leopard successfully tagged, the team is hopeful its mission will be a success, and the team members will be charting their progress for the BBC News website.

SEE ALSO
▸ Snow leopard fitted with GPS tag
27 Nov 06 | Technology

RELATED INTERNET LINKS
▸ Snow Leopard Trust
▸ WWF Pakistan
The BBC is not responsible for the content of external internet sites

TOP TECHNOLOGY STORIES
▸ iPhone court battle put on hold
▸ Word works with open file styles
▸ Vista has speech recognition hole
▸ News feeds

MOST POPULAR STORIES NOW
MOST E-MAILED   MOST READ
1 Top Gear insulting, says charity
2 C4 postpones masturbation season

**T**his BBC News site reports on the Snow Leopard Trust's GPS-collaring project in the Chitral-Gol National Park on the Pakistan-Afghanistan border. A diary kept by Dr. Tom McCarthy gives readers an inside look at this tracking project.

*Access this Web site from http://www.myreportlinks.com*

shrublands, grasslands, and steppe vegetation in China, deserts in Mongolia, and coniferous forests. They usually range from 9,800 to 14,800 feet (3,000 to 4,500 meters) above sea level. Snow leopards have been sighted at up to 18,400 feet (5,520 meters), probably traveling over passes, since there is not much food at such an altitude, and as low as 2,800 feet (840 meters) above sea level.

Snow leopards have surprisingly varied home-range territories, depending on terrain and available food. In the 1980s, Rodney Jackson and Gary Ahlborn discovered that one radio-collared animal in a prey-rich area of India had a home range of just 5 square miles (13 square kilometers). In 1999, Dr. Tom McCarthy of the International Snow Leopard Trust tracked a radio-collared snow leopard in Mongolia over a range of nearly 1,200 square kilometers (463 square miles), in an area where prey was scarce.

## ▶ Marking Territory

Unlike other big cats around the world, such as the endangered Florida panther, adult male snow leopards do not usually battle each other over their territories. In fact their territories may often overlap, something that is very unusual for big cats. Certain popular hunting grounds are even shared by a number of snow leopards. But battles do occur when a young male tries to take over a dominant male's territories. The animals' instincts for marking territory help to keep such battles to a minimum, however. The snow leopards leave scented "calling cards" for each other, to warn away potential rivals. They do this by scuffing the ground with their paws or leaving behind visible scrapes. They also urinate on rock faces. Many of the world's big cats mark their territories in this way. Territory marking increases in winter and early spring when the animals mate. Scientists think this is done so that males can attract females, while keeping other males at a distance. The female's scent contains information for the males about her readiness to breed.

## ▶ Snow Leopard Range

The snow leopard's range is thinly spread over a vast area of tall mountain ranges in Central Asia. These mountain ranges include the Hindu Kush of Afghanistan, the Himalayas, the Pamirs, the Tien Shans, the Altai, and the Sayan Mountains.

The snow leopard's range extends for more than 1 million square miles (nearly 3 million square kilometers), though it occupies significant habitat in only about 617,763 square miles (1.6 million square kilometers). It is found in twelve countries: Afghanistan, Bhutan, China, India, Mongolia,

Nepal, Pakistan, Russia, Kazakhstan, Kyrgyzstan, Tajikistan, and Uzbekistan.

## ▶ Snow Leopard Populations

How many snow leopards are left in the world? No one really knows, but scientists think there may be between 4,000 and 7,000 animals. Snow leopards are so elusive, and there have been so few population surveys in the difficult mountain terrain where they live, that it is impossible to know the exact number of animals currently alive. The International Snow Leopard Trust, however, uses the following numbers in their estimates of snow leopard populations.

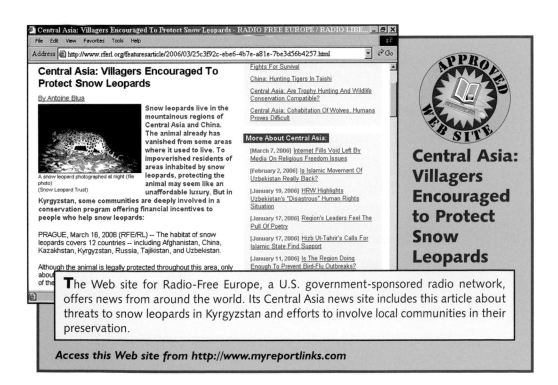

The Web site for Radio-Free Europe, a U.S. government-sponsored radio network, offers news from around the world. Its Central Asia news site includes this article about threats to snow leopards in Kyrgyzstan and efforts to involve local communities in their preservation.

*Access this Web site from http://www.myreportlinks.com*

## ▶ Afghanistan and Bhutan

There are an unknown number of snow leopards in Afghanistan, living in the Hindu Kush mountain range. The size of the habitat suggests that the region might support 100 to 200 animals. War and the resulting poverty there have undoubtedly reduced that number.

No population survey has been done in Bhutan, but scientists estimate around 100 snow leopards to be living in the northern parts of the country bordering Tibet, where the Jigme Dorji National Park and the Kulong Chhu Wildlife Sanctuary provide protection for the animals.

## ▶ China, Mongolia, and India

China has the largest remaining population of snow leopards, with an estimated 2,000 to 2,500 animals. They are found in the western mountain ranges of Inner Mongolia, in the Tibet and Xinjiang Autonomous Regions, and in the provinces of Qinghai, Gansu, Sichuan, Yunnan, and Shanxi. Field surveys have found that the historic range of snow leopards in China continues to shrink and that the animals may be on the brink of extinction in Inner Mongolia.

Mongolia's population of 1,000 snow leopards lives mostly in mountainous regions in the western part of the country. Though the cat population is relatively high there, it is scattered and fragmented,

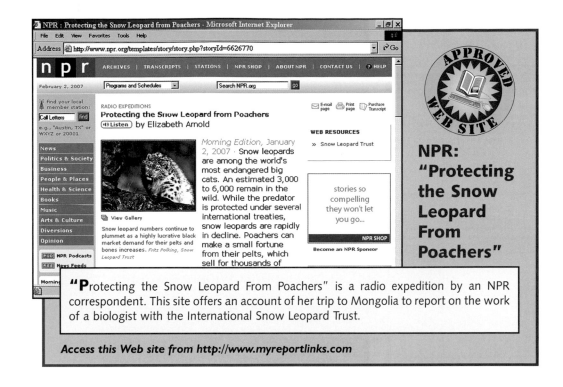

NPR: "Protecting the Snow Leopard From Poachers"

"Protecting the Snow Leopard From Poachers" is a radio expedition by an NPR correspondent. This site offers an account of her trip to Mongolia to report on the work of a biologist with the International Snow Leopard Trust.

*Access this Web site from http://www.myreportlinks.com*

which leaves open the constant threat of local extinctions.

In India, the snow leopard is found in the Himalayan region. There are between 200 and 600 of the big cats in India, with the largest number in central Ladakh, in the state of Jammu and Kashmir. The population survey in India was conducted in 1991, however, so it is not known how many of the big cats live in India today.

## ▶ Russia and Former Soviet Republics

Russia is thought to have just between 50 and 150 snow leopards left, with much of the animal's historic range now empty of the big cat. In what was once snow leopard habitat, some forests have been cleared and people have moved in, putting great pressure on the remaining snow leopards.

In countries that were once part of the Soviet Union, the cats are faring somewhat better, for the most part. Kyrgyzstan, a former Soviet republic, is home to between 800 and 1,400 snow leopards. There may be 120 to 300 snow leopards in Tajikistan, mostly in the mountains in the eastern part of the country. Kazakhstan has a population of 180 to 200 snow leopards widely scattered in mountain ranges in the northern, eastern, and southeastern parts of the country. This estimate, though, was made in 1990, and it is thought that the population has declined since then. But in Uzbekistan, only between 10 and 50 snow leopards remain, in the eastern part of the country.

## ▶ Nepal and Pakistan

Between 350 and 500 snow leopards are found in the Himalayan Mountains of Nepal. The big cat is found in the Manang District in western Nepal and in the Mugu and Dolpa districts of the far west. There are also eight protected areas in Nepal for the snow leopards. Recent reports have the cats returning to Sagarmatha (Everest) National Park and the Annapurna Conservation Area, including Manang, where the cats were filmed over a twelve-year period by a Japanese crew, and

CNN.com: Snow Leopards Spotted on Top of World

**This** article from CNN describes a graduate student's sighting in 2004 of a snow leopard on the southern slopes of Mount Everest. Scientists had not seen the species there in more than forty years. Learn more about the cat's recovery "at the top of the world."

*Access this Web site from http://www.myreportlinks.com*

Mustang, where the Snow Leopard Conservancy has a livestock corral improvement program.

Pakistan may have between 250 to 420 snow leopards, scattered over a vast area of 31,274 square miles (81,000 square kilometers). This is where George Schaller first encountered snow leopards in 1970 and where, sadly, four years later, he found very few. But since the 1970s, community-based conservation efforts have brightened the snow leopard's outlook in that country. In 2005, villagers in Hushey, in northern Pakistan's Karakoram Mountains, received a Disney Conservation Hero Award for releasing a snow leopard that had been trapped in a livestock pen. (The award is given each

In the wild, snow leopard cubs are usually dependent upon their mothers for nearly two years. Scientists have yet to witness a cub's birth in the wild.

year by the Disney Wildlife Conservation Fund to five local people or communities committed to conserving wildlife in their corner of the world.)

It is important to remember that these population figures by country are only very rough estimates. They are based on direct observation of the animals, their tracks, dead snow leopards found, sales of furs, collecting of snow leopard cubs, and other evidence. This data is valuable, but not conclusive. Scientists are coming up with new methods and technologies to better track the cats so that population figures can more accurately reflect their numbers in each country. But as conservationists warn, it takes more than knowing how many snow leopards are left to truly save them. More community-based conservation in partnership with the local people remains the species' best hope for survival.

## ▶Reproduction

In his book *The Last Big Cats*, wildlife photographer Erwin A. Bauer notes that almost everything scientists know about snow leopard mating behavior comes from observing the animals in zoos. No one has ever been able to stay close enough to a wild adult snow leopard to fully track its reproductive habits.

It is known that mating occurs in winter, between December and March, throughout Central

Asia. There is a 90- to 100-day gestation period, and an average of one to three cubs are born in each litter. Cubs are born in April, May, and June, after the worst winter weather has subsided. This ensures that food is abundant and that there will be less effort needed for a mother snow leopard to secure a kill and protect her young from the cold.

Snow leopards are born blind, with their eyes closed. Newborns weigh between 0.7 to 1.56 pounds (320 to 708 grams) at birth. The mother lines her natal den, the place where she will give birth, with her own fur to protect the newborns from severe cold. Even so, it is still believed that cub mortality is high.

The young are dependent on their mothers for about two years. The animals reach sexual maturity at two or three years of age. In captivity, snow leopards have been known to live for twenty-one years. It is believed that the animals rarely get that old in the wild, though, since conditions are much harsher there. No one really knows how long snow leopards can live in the wild.

## ▶ Myth and Legends About the Elusive Cat

As long as it has roamed the mountains of Central Asia, the snow leopard has inspired stories that have become the stuff of legends. These myths, passed down orally from one generation to the next, were told and retold around campfires and

For some people of the Himalayas, snow leopards are still considered spirits of the mountain, imbued with mystical powers, as this painting suggests.

the family hearth. The stories vary depending on their country of origin.

One of the stories from Tibet is about Milarepa, an eleventh-century Buddhist saint, who traveled throughout what is today the Qomolangma Nature Preserve. There he would meditate in small caves and tiny mountain villages. After staying for a time in one such village, he decided to return to the Great Cave of Conquering Demons to be alone. The villagers thought it would be helpful to have this demon conqueror in their community, so they begged Milarepa to stay with

National Geographic Adventure Mag.: Searching for snow leopards in Ladakh, India with award-win - Mi...

File   Edit   View   Favorites   Tools   Help

Address http://www.nationalgeographic.com/adventure/0508/photo_01.html   Go

Photo Gallery                                                              Next >>
### Searching for Snow Leopards

**More Related Sites**

**Rare Snow Leopard**
Learn more about the snow leopard and see how new measures are being developed to track its population.

**Snow Leopard Conservancy**
Check out more photos of the cats in their natural habitat and learn more about Rodney Jackson's effort to them.

"This was taken very early on when the team first got together. Wildlife biologist Rodney Jackson is tying a *kata*, Buddhist scarf, to bring us all good luck. I was never superstitious before I came to India, but now some four years later I am very much so. Ironically, this is around the same spot where sculptor Mark Coreth later spotted a snow leopard."

*National Geographic Adventure:* **Searching for Snow Leopards** is the story of a photographer and a writer who brave the mountains of northwestern India with Rodney Jackson, pictured, and others to find snow leopards. In this photograph, Jackson bows to the superstitions of the land as he ties a kata, a Buddhist scarf that is supposed to bring good luck.

them for the winter, but he refused. He promised, however, to give instruction to any villager who was able to climb up the mountain to find him.

That winter, it snowed for eighteen days and nights in one stretch, and the path to the cave was cut off from the village for six months, so no one could reach Milarepa. When the snows melted in the spring and the trail to the cave was finally clear, the villagers were sure that Milarepa must have died in the brutal cold. They performed certain rituals to honor his memory. Then they went in search of his body.

Stopping to rest just before reaching the cave, they saw a snow leopard in the distance on a rock, yawning and stretching its legs. They were more sure than ever that Milarepa was dead, killed and eaten by this snow leopard. Then they noticed human tracks beside the snow leopard's tracks, and as they approached the Great Cave of Conquering Demons, they were astonished to find Milarepa alive, and singing. When they asked Milarepa how he had survived the snow and the big cat, he laughed and told them that he had transformed himself into that cat—he was the snow leopard they had seen![7]

## ▶ Snow Leopards and Mountain Spirits

People believe not only that the snow leopard helps saints but that it also magically comes to the aid of common people. Dr. John Mock, lecturer in Hindi and Urdu languages at the University of California at Santa Cruz and a scholar of Pakistani folklore, retells a story from Pakistan about the snow leopard. It seems that a man went into the high mountains to hunt. He stayed there overnight and was awakened by something heavy sitting on him. It was a snow leopard, but not any ordinary snow leopard. It was a mountain spirit known as a *pari,* disguised as a snow leopard. Ever afterward, that pari came to the man and was friends with him. In a story told by the hunter's son, "Whenever he was preparing to hunt somewhere, that pari said to him at night in a dream . . . 'In such and such place go and hunt. To such and such place don't go and hunt, no game is there.' Whether ibex, or whether small game, he would go and it would be there. Such miraculous things happened with him," until the end of his life.[8]

Some beliefs actually help to preserve the snow leopard. In the Dolpo region of Nepal, there are stories of lamas, or Tibetan Buddhist monks, who transformed themselves into snow leopards to travel over the steep mountains to Tibet to find herbs used as medicine. The people of Dolpo will not kill snow leopards because they still believe that the big cats (as well as domestic cats) were born to remove their past sins. By killing a snow leopard, the animal's sins are transferred to the person who has killed it.[9]

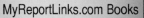

# THREATS TO THE SPECIES

**Like** most endangered species, snow leopards face a multitude of major threats. Their habitat is diminishing and becoming fragmented because the human population in their range is growing. The big cats also face the loss of their natural prey, which leads them to sometimes kill domestic livestock for food, pitting them against herders and farmers who retaliate and kill them. Snow leopards are hunted, poisoned, and poached as pests as well as for their pelts. Their meat and bones are illegally used in Chinese and Tibetan medicine. Climate change caused by global warming, which brings with it the rapid melting of glaciers in the high mountains, may also have a negative impact on the last remaining snow leopards.

## ▶ Habitat Loss and Fragmentation

The world's population of people, now 6.4 billion, more than quadrupled in the twentieth century, putting tremendous pressure on Earth's wild animals. Global population could top 9 billion by

SNOW LEOPARD PHOTO GALLERY

© ROBERT TRAWICK                                              WWW.THEBIGCATS.COM

Done

**T**he Big Cats—Snow Leopard is a Web page providing a brief fact sheet on snow leopards, a map showing the cats' distribution, and more than thirty images of this big cat species, including this one.

2050, according to the United Nations, putting even more pressure on wildlife.

Human population is growing especially fast in some of the developing countries where the snow leopard is found. Today, China and India are the most heavily populated nations in the world, with Pakistan the sixth most heavily populated country on Earth. These three countries are also the fastest growing in the world today. According to a United Nations Population Division study forecasting growth within thirty years of 1995,

India's population will increase by an additional 401 million people by 2025. China will grow by 260 million. Pakistan will come in third, with a population expected to grow by about 133 million.[1]

The population growth in these countries, and in the other nine countries in which the snow leopard lives, means that more homes will be built, more roads carved out of mountains, and especially more agricultural lands developed to feed that population. While we may think of the snow leopard as living in the most remote and rugged parts of the world, it is fast losing its habitat to the activities of people, especially in alpine livestock pastures where domestic sheep, goats, and cattle are herded. In China and other Asian countries experiencing rapid growth, increased use of oil and gas as well as mining and deforestation are also changing the landscape drastically and having a profound effect on the countries' wildlife populations.

The snow leopard's habitat is also threatened by another human activity: war. The fighting in Afghanistan and northern India and Pakistan infringes on the snow leopard's territory and threatens its safety.

## Loss of Prey

Imagine going to the supermarket and finding a little less food on the shelves each day. Then imagine

▲ *What does the future hold for a young snow leopard cub like this? Will it even have a habitat to call home twenty years from now?*

that you went to other supermarkets in the area and they too had less and less food to sell. In a very short time, you and your neighbors would find yourselves competing for what little food was left. If things did not get better, those people who could not compete for the last available food would begin to starve. Hungry people can be driven to steal food, resulting in punishment if caught.

## ▶ Driven to Steal

Hungry snow leopards face a similar situation: The decline of their natural prey is a huge threat to the species. The animals the cats eat—wild goats, sheep, and small mammals such as marmots—are vanishing throughout the snow leopard's range. Those prey species are being diminished as human populations grow. People and their domestic livestock take over the alpine meadows where the prey species once grazed and lived. Prey species are unable to compete with domestic livestock and must therefore leave in search of more grasses, or die. They are also hunted (in the case of wild sheep) or poisoned (in the case of marmots). The snow leopards are left with little choice but to go hungry or prey on the newly introduced livestock. The people whose lives depend on this livestock cannot tolerate these snow leopard attacks, and they hunt down and kill the cats.

Madan Oli, a Nepalese zoologist, was the first scientist to document this problem when he did research in 1987 in the upper Marsyangdi Valley of the Manang district of Nepal. Madan Oli interviewed herders and farmers in the region and learned a grim truth. A third of those he talked with had experienced livestock losses to snow leopards between 1989 and 1990. Over that time, they lost about 3 percent of their livestock to snow leopard kills. Not surprisingly, the farmers and herders had no love for the big cats since the animals were threatening their livelihoods. An amazing 87 percent of the households favored hunting down and killing all snow leopards as

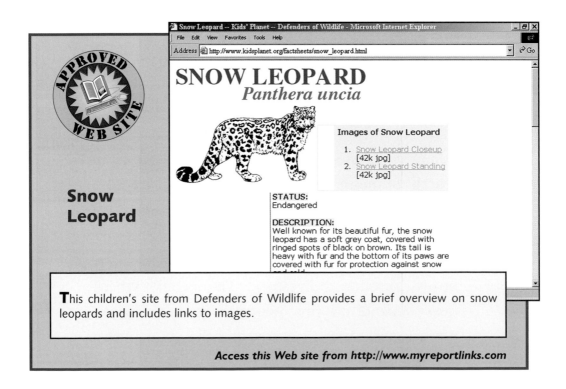

This children's site from Defenders of Wildlife provides a brief overview on snow leopards and includes links to images.

*Access this Web site from http://www.myreportlinks.com*

soon as possible. It did not really matter much that their nation had designated the snow leopard an endangered species. In fact, snow leopard poachers were quietly honored as heroes by their communities.[2] At the time, conservation groups had not yet begun to work with the community to encourage snow leopard conservation.

## Economic Survival

When it came to the survival of their own families versus the survival of snow leopards, the farmers and herders logically chose their families. In India's Kibber Wildlife Sanctuary, it was found that 18 percent of all villagers' livestock was killed by snow leopards and wolves, with an estimated total value of $128 per household per year. When an average household's income is only $200 to $400 per year, it is easy to see why people feel they have little choice but to kill the attacking snow leopards.

The number of domestic livestock killed has grown in recent years because the animals often must go unprotected by herders. Children who used to do much of the daytime herding are now going to school. Many teenagers choose not to continue their family's herding lifestyle and leave their small villages to find work in the cities. In the Annapurna/Mustang region of Nepal, it is becoming more common for several families to hire a herder to stay on the pastures with their livestock.

Some people have become more tolerant of the loss of their cattle and other livestock to hungry snow leopards. Villagers living near Hemis National Park in the Ladakh division of the northern Indian state of Jammu and Kashmir often see snow leopards but do not usually harm them, at least not anymore. Darla Hillard of the Snow Leopard Conservancy explains that her group "has worked intensively with these Buddhist communities for the past six years, on corral predator-proofing, Himalayan Homestay development, and school-based educational activities. Because they are no longer losing livestock in their improved pens, and because they see financial benefits in protecting the cats, they are better able to tolerate the occasional loss of livestock. And they have told us that they are happy that they can be better Buddhists."[3]

## Poaching and Hunting

In the past, the hunting of snow leopards for their pelts and the capture of the animals for zoos, museums, and private collections may have had the biggest impact on the species' population. It is thought that the world trade in snow leopard skins from Russia alone in the 1920s came to a staggering one thousand pelts per year. Around the world, snow leopard pelts were even presented as official gifts between national leaders.

**SILENT ROAR** : Searching for the Snow Leopard

Featured Program

Acclaimed wildlife filmmakers capture the first intimate portrait of the world's most elusive cat.

Most big cats do their best to remain hidden from human eyes, but none are quite as adept at this as the snow leopard. These cats lead largely solitary lives, populating the Himalayas at altitudes that offer only about half the oxygen to which humans are accustomed. So when wildlife filmmakers Hugh Miles and Mitchell Kelly set out to film this animal they knew they were in for a challenge.

VIDEO

The filmmakers chose Hemis National Park in the northern Indian state of Jammu and Kashmir as their base camp. There they selected a team of native mountaineers and trackers to accompany them into the Himalayas. The team climbed as high as 15,000 feet, tracking the cats via paw prints in the snow and the scented urine that snow leopards use to mark their

SPECIAL FEATURES

Protecting the Elusive Cat
More on Rodney Jackson's work.

Life at the Edge of the World
The people of the Himalayas.

Behind the Scenes
Meet filmmaker Mitchell Kelly.

Done

**APPROVED WEB SITE**

**NATURE:**
**Silent Roar:**
**Searching**
**for the Snow**
**Leopard**

**T**his Web site, a companion to the PBS documentary *Silent Roar: Searching for the Snow Leopard*, profiles Dr. Rodney Jackson's efforts to find and save snow leopards in the Himalayas. Additional photographs and resources are also found on this site.

**EDITOR'S CHOICE**

*Access this Web site from http://www.myreportlinks.com*

Since 1975, the Convention on International Trade in Endangered Species of Wild Fauna and Flora (CITES) has done much to help curb this illegal trade.

Unfortunately, no one knows how many snow leopards are lost each year to hunting and poaching. What is known is that it is not difficult to kill a snow leopard. Though the animals are generally shy, they seem to have no fear of guns or approaching people. Erwin A. Bauer tells of one hunter who fired three times at a snow leopard, leaving the animal completely unafraid as it returned to its kill to eat. A trekking guide told Bauer that his group of a dozen hikers once came

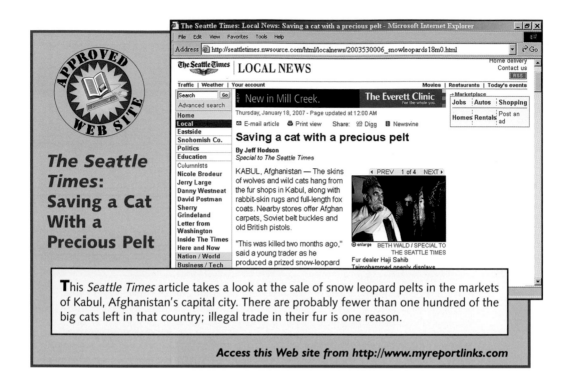

The Seattle
Times:
Saving a Cat
With a
Precious Pelt

**The Seattle Times: Local News: Saving a cat with a precious pelt** - Microsoft Internet Explorer

Address http://seattletimes.nwsource.com/html/localnews/2003530006_snowleopards18m0.html

**The Seattle Times** | **LOCAL NEWS**

Traffic | Weather | Your account          Movies | Restaurants | Today's events

New in Mill Creek.          The Everett Clinic
For the whole you.

Thursday, January 18, 2007 - Page updated at 12:00 AM

E-mail article    Print view    Share: Digg    Newsvine

**Saving a cat with a precious pelt**

By Jeff Hodson
Special to The Seattle Times

KABUL, Afghanistan — The skins
of wolves and wild cats hang from
the fur shops in Kabul, along with
rabbit-skin rugs and full-length fox
coats. Nearby stores offer Afghan
carpets, Soviet belt buckles and
old British pistols.

"This was killed two months ago,"
said a young trader as he
produced a prized snow-leopard

‹ PREV   1 of 4   NEXT ›

enlarge   BETH WALD / SPECIAL TO
THE SEATTLE TIMES
Fur dealer Haji Sahib
Taimohammed openly displays

Jobs | Autos | Shopping

Homes | Rentals   Post an
ad

This *Seattle Times* article takes a look at the sale of snow leopard pelts in the markets of Kabul, Afghanistan's capital city. There are probably fewer than one hundred of the big cats left in that country; illegal trade in their fur is one reason.

**Access this Web site from http://www.myreportlinks.com**

within 30 feet (9 meters) of a crouching snow leopard who was undisturbed and unfrightened by their passage.[4]

Though the trading of snow leopard pelts is illegal in all twelve nations in which the species lives, the pelts are still being sold. A study by the World Wildlife Fund documents a sharp rise in the hunting of snow leopards in the 1990s for furs as well as for the Chinese medicine trade. The war in Afghanistan has made it easier to trade snow leopard skins. "Snow leopard pelts can sell for as much as $1,000 in Kabul [the capital of Afghanistan], which is more than double what a herder there makes in a year," according to Tom Dillon, director of species conservation at the World Wildlife Fund. "That's a powerful incentive to kill Afghanistan's dwindling population of cats."[5]

In June 1990, police in China's Qinghai province confiscated forty snow leopard pelts stored at a taxidermist's house. In December 1999, three dealers of snow leopard pelts in China's Fujian province who had been caught with seventeen skins were sentenced to five to eight years in prison for their crime. In the Sichuan province, snow leopard is still reportedly sold as an exotic dish to tourists and residents. There are many other examples of poachers caught killing the big cats or people selling their pelts and meat.

## Illegal Sales

Public advertisements for the snow leopards' skins have even turned up in newspapers and on the Internet, although such sales are strictly forbidden by law. According to the World Wildlife Fund study mentioned earlier, "A Snow Leopard skin rug was offered for sale in the *Jakarta Post,* an Indonesian daily newspaper in English, in September 2001. . . . and the German Society for Nature Conservation (NABU) reported a Snow Leopard skin coat [priced at USD100] and stuffed Snow Leopard advertised on *e-bay,* an internet-based trading site, in November 2002 and March 2003."[6]

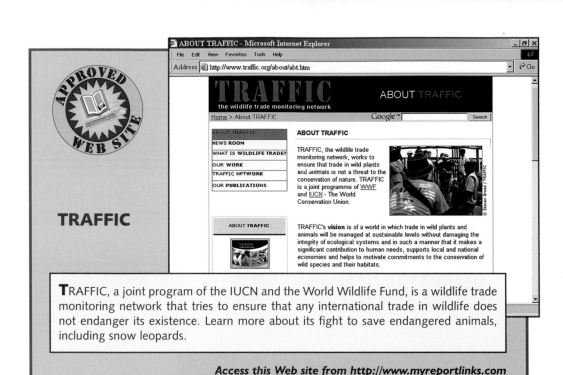

TRAFFIC, a joint program of the IUCN and the World Wildlife Fund, is a wildlife trade monitoring network that tries to ensure that any international trade in wildlife does not endanger its existence. Learn more about its fight to save endangered animals, including snow leopards.

*Access this Web site from http://www.myreportlinks.com*

It is easy to understand why people continue to risk prison by trading snow leopard pelts and body parts: The value of a snow leopard skin is currently more than sixty times the minimum yearly wage in some of the countries where the animals live.

## ▷ Snow Leopards and the Illegal Chinese Medicine Trade

There is an increased demand for snow leopard bones in the Chinese medicine trade. This surge came about when the world's nations cracked down on the illegal trade in tiger bones, which had also been used in many of the traditional medicines of Asia. Snow leopard bones have been used for centuries in medicines to treat rheumatism, tendonitis, and bone fractures. The powdered bone of the big cat is supposed to decrease inflammation and relieve pain. The skulls of snow leopards have also been used in religious healing rituals in Nepal and China. Other body parts that are sold through this illegal medicine trade include the cats' sex organs, teeth, claws, and skin.

Though the penalties for killing or trading the body parts of snow leopards are severe, the hunters and poachers responsible rarely get convicted because the big cats' deaths are rarely reported.

## ▶Climate Change

Like many of the world's endangered species, the snow leopard is also being threatened by climate change. Snow leopards usually live between 9,800 and 14,800 feet (3,000 and 4,500 meters) above sea level, between the tree line and the permanent snow line.

But as the world warms, the high altitude ecosystem is changing. The tree line and snow line are retreating ever higher into the mountains due to global warming. Rising temperatures and a receding snow line are forcing snow leopards to move higher and higher into the mountains, where vegetation and the wild animals that the big cats feed on are scarcer. In other areas of the

Kashmir goats in Ladakh, India (also home to the snow leopard). The wool from these goats is prized for its softness and is used to make expensive clothing. Climate change may affect domestic animals differently than wild ones.

snow leopard's range, the melting of glaciers and increased rainfall could actually help the plant-eating animals such as sheep and goats that the snow leopards live on. The issue of climate change is a complex one, requiring more attention, as an official of Nepal's Department of National Parks and Wildlife Conservation points out: "Since climate change is a reality which impacts the habitat, snow leopards may get affected by the phenomena. But we cannot say anything definite as we have not conducted enough studies on the issue."[7]

# PROTECTING THE SNOW LEOPARD

**Though** known to the people of Central Asia for thousands of years, the snow leopard was not known to the Western world until 1761. That year, a French naturalist named Count Georges Buffon first published a book containing a drawing that closely resembled a snow leopard.

In 1891, the first-ever captive snow leopard outside Asia arrived at the London Zoo, and another was sent as a gift to the United States in 1903. That animal's life ended tragically when it escaped from the New York Zoological Park, better known as the Bronx Zoo, and was shot by a New York City policeman.

Despite these early proofs of the snow leopard's existence, some people still did not believe it existed. Author Richard Lydekker in his 1907 book *The Game Animals of India, Burma, Malaya and Tibet,* even went so far as to deny the existence of what many people called the "ghost cat."

It was not until the 1970s when George B. Schaller photographed the snow leopard that the rest of the world began to really take an interest in

▲ Snow leopards have been known as the "ghost cats" of the Himalayas for many years because they are so difficult to find in their high mountain habitat.

the animal. By this time, the species was seriously endangered. The wild sheep and wild goats, the prey animals that the snow leopard relied on for its food, were becoming scarce. The animal's skins were highly valued to make coats and hats. And the big cat's bones were often being used in Chinese medicine.

To research the snow leopard, Schaller had to be more than a wildlife biologist. He had to be an athlete and outdoorsman, living and climbing in the harsh high-altitude world of the big cats. His dedication paid off. He became the first known person to photograph and film the snow leopard in the wild. He was also able to track a female snow leopard for twenty-eight hours over a week. Schaller went on to write about his experiences with the snow leopard in *Stones of Silence: Journeys in the Himalaya,* which helped to bring the snow leopard into the forefront of the world conservation community.

## ▶ International Protection

One of the threats to the snow leopard is illegal trade in its pelts and other body parts. That is why the snow leopard's listing in CITES as an Appendix I animal is so important. CITES is an international agreement between governments that works to ensure that the survival of wild animals and plants is not threatened by international trade.[1] Roughly

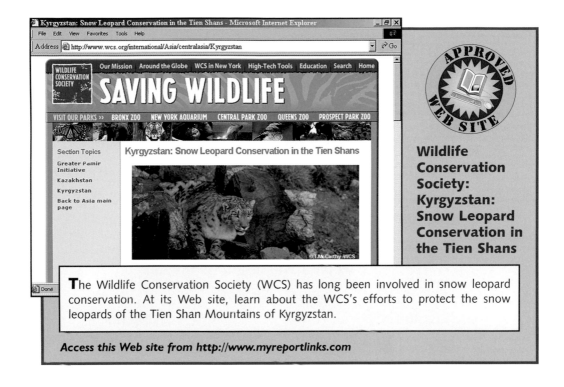

Kyrgyzstan: Snow Leopard Conservation in the Tien Shans - Microsoft Internet Explorer

File  Edit  View  Favorites  Tools  Help

Address  http://www.wcs.org/international/Asia/centralasia/Kyrgyzstan

**WILDLIFE CONSERVATION SOCIETY**
Our Mission  Around the Globe  WCS in New York  High-Tech Tools  Education  Search  Home

**SAVING WILDLIFE**

VISIT OUR PARKS >>  BRONX ZOO  NEW YORK AQUARIUM  CENTRAL PARK ZOO  QUEENS ZOO  PROSPECT PARK ZOO

Section Topics

Greater Pamir Initiative

Kazakhstan

Kyrgyzstan

Back to Asia main page

Kyrgyzstan: Snow Leopard Conservation in the Tien Shans

© T. McCarthy /WCS

**Wildlife Conservation Society: Kyrgyzstan: Snow Leopard Conservation in the Tien Shans**

The Wildlife Conservation Society (WCS) has long been involved in snow leopard conservation. At its Web site, learn about the WCS's efforts to protect the snow leopards of the Tien Shan Mountains of Kyrgyzstan.

*Access this Web site from http://www.myreportlinks.com*

five thousand species of animals and twenty-eight thousand species of plants are protected by CITES against such trade.

This treaty not only attempts to prevent the trading of snow leopard skins between nations but it also seeks to control the capture of live animals for zoos. Appendix I species are the ones considered most endangered and most threatened with extinction. Under Appendix I, all trade of these animals either living or dead is forbidden, except under rare exceptional circumstances such as for scientific research. All of the countries in which the snow leopard lives except Kyrgyzstan and Tajikistan are members of CITES. This international agreement, however, is only binding on those countries that voluntarily agree to be part of it. It is up to the individual nations to enact laws to protect the wildlife in their lands. As a result, enforcement of the treaty can only go so far. Between 1975 and 2000, only three seizures of clothing made from snow leopard skins were made under the treaty. Certainly, many more animal skins were turned into garments over that time, though the people killing, trading in, and wearing the animal pelts were not caught.

The snow leopard was listed as an Appendix I species of the United Nations Convention on Migratory Species (CMS) in 1985 and was upgraded in 2002 to a Concerted Action Species. The CMS

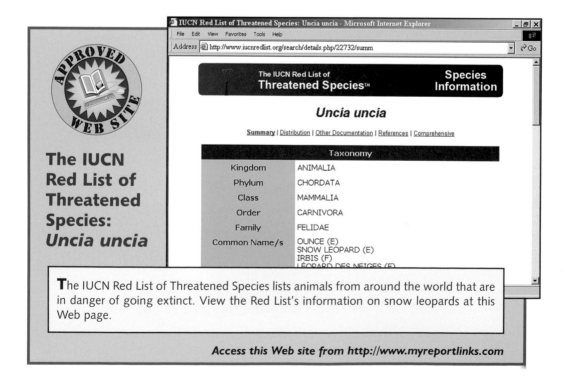

**The IUCN Red List of Threatened Species: Uncia uncia**

The IUCN Red List of Threatened Species lists animals from around the world that are in danger of going extinct. View the Red List's information on snow leopards at this Web page.

*Access this Web site from http://www.myreportlinks.com*

"aims to conserve terrestrial, marine, and avian migratory species throughout their range. . . . Migratory species threatened with extinction are listed on Appendix I of the Convention. CMS Parties strive towards strictly protecting these animals, conserving or restoring the places where they live, mitigating obstacles to migration and controlling other factors that might endanger them."[2] But only five nations within the snow leopard's range—India, Mongolia, Pakistan, Tajikistan, and Uzbekistan—have signed the CMS agreement so far.

The snow leopard is also listed with the IUCN-World Conservation Union, an important international organization that monitors the world's animal species. The snow leopard is listed on the IUCN's Red List, which contains animals that are critically endangered, endangered, vulnerable, threatened, of least concern, or are data deficient. The Red List currently considers the snow leopard to be endangered throughout its range.

## National Protections

The earliest national protections for the snow leopard came during the 1960s in the former Soviet Union when the government became concerned over the declining number of snow leopard furs that were available to trappers. Limits on the hunting and capture of the big cats were put in place in Kazakhstan, then part of the Soviet Union. This had little impact on the hunting of the animals though, since "wearing a leopard-skin cap and jacket was long a symbol of daring, bravery, and authority in mountainous rural Asia."[3]

Since then the snow leopard has been given nationwide legal protection in all twelve of its range countries. However, laws alone are seldom enough to truly protect an endangered species. The laws must be enforced for them to work. And in nearly all of the dozen range countries, snow leopard protections are poorly enforced, leaving the big cats vulnerable. Also, while these laws often forbid hunting, poaching, and trading of skins, they do not limit the growth of human population or of domestic herds, both threats to the species.

## ▶ Setting Aside Parklands

One strategy that has worked extremely well for protecting endangered species is the preservation of critical habitat—territory sufficient in size for an animal to carry out all the activities of its life. Saving critical habitat for a species like the American crocodile has been very effective, since this animal lives in a fairly small home range. But saving enough critical habitat to conserve the snow leopard would be far more difficult. A great deal of land is needed to protect this big cat at the top of the food chain. Enough critical habitat

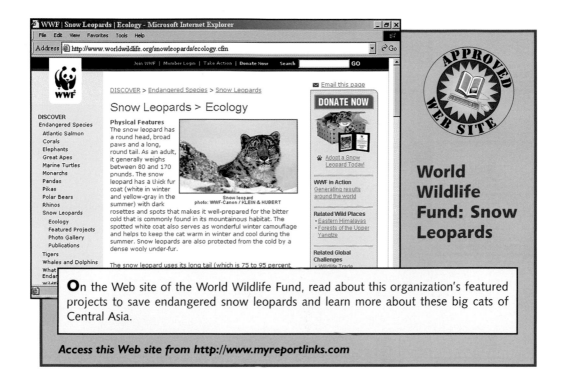

Join WWF | Member Login | Take Action | Donate Now   Search   GO

✉ Email this page

DISCOVER > Endangered Species > Snow Leopards

## Snow Leopards > Ecology

DISCOVER
Endangered Species
Atlantic Salmon
Corals
Elephants
Great Apes
Marine Turtles
Monarchs
Pandas
Pikas
Polar Bears
Rhinos
Snow Leopards
   Ecology
   Featured Projects
   Photo Gallery
   Publications
Tigers
Whales and Dolphins
What
Endan
wilds

**Physical Features**
The snow leopard has a round head, broad paws and a long, round tail. As an adult, it generally weighs between 80 and 170 pounds. The snow leopard has a thick fur coat (white in winter and yellow-gray in the summer) with dark rosettes and spots that makes it well-prepared for the bitter cold that is commonly found in its mountainous habitat. The spotted white coat also serves as wonderful winter camouflage and helps to keep the cat warm in winter and cool during the summer. Snow leopards are also protected from the cold by a dense wooly under-fur.

The snow leopard uses its long tail (which is 75 to 95 percent

Snow leopard
photo: WWF-Canon / KLEIN & HUBERT

**DONATE NOW**

🐾 Adopt a Snow
   Leopard Today!

**WWF in Action**
Generating results
around the world

**Related Wild Places**
• Eastern Himalayas
• Forests of the Upper
  Yangtze

**Related Global
Challenges**
• Wildlife Trade

**World
Wildlife
Fund: Snow
Leopards**

**O**n the Web site of the World Wildlife Fund, read about this organization's featured projects to save endangered snow leopards and learn more about these big cats of Central Asia.

*Access this Web site from http://www.myreportlinks.com*

needs to be protected not only for the animals themselves but also for the large and small prey they need to live.

Parkland preservation for snow leopards is hard to justify in developing nations such as Pakistan and India where the human population is growing remarkably fast. Many of the people in those countries need every acre of ground they can get for farming or grazing, to feed their families. Most of the twelve nations in which the snow leopard lives have created preserves that partially protect snow leopards. Many of these parks are too small to do much good, however.

▲ *A snow leopard trails its long tail in a river. Scientists have withstood harsh and even life-threatening conditions to catch a glimpse of these elusive cats.*

Researcher Jan-Olov Andersson reports in a scientific paper that only two protected areas within the snow leopard's entire range are large enough to accommodate viable snow leopard populations. The two largest reserves, located in China, are not even as useful as they might be, since much snow leopard range still lies outside the boundaries of the two parks. "[I]t will be difficult to save the snow leopard if we would have to rely on protected areas only," says Andersson.[4]

## Continued Research

In 1981, Rodney Jackson and Darla Hillard traveled to one of the most remote and rugged regions on Earth, the Langu Gorge region of western Nepal, to study snow leopards. Another scientist, Gary Ahlborn, joined them in 1983. The scientists and Hillard faced tremendous hardships in their work. They had to carry all of their tents, gear, and scientific equipment to the study site on foot, a journey that took ten days. The first year they were there, Jackson and Hillard endured one of the worst winters ever in the region, with storms so fierce they were snowbound for the first seven weeks. Finally they were able to set out a wire snare baited with a live goat, in the hopes of capturing a snow leopard.

> Miraculously, the next morning the trap held a leopard. Twenty minutes after tranquilizing it, the world's first radio-collared snow leopard walked away. Six more months passed before the

▲ *A steep cliff's ledge remains a favorite place for a snow leopard to rest. The habitat of these big cats poses difficulties for those trying to study them, although improved technology has helped scientists track snow leopards more closely from afar.*

biologists captured the second of five they caught altogether. What they learned during four years of [radio] tracking these animals over the mountain terrain turned the danger and terrible hardships into high adventure and a hugely rewarding experience, both professionally and personally.[5]

The information gained by radio-tracking confirmed what George Schaller had learned the hard way—by tracking afoot and with binoculars and spotting scopes: The snow leopards preferred the most broken and difficult terrain, especially cliffs. Like other big cats around the world, they used the cliffs to make their daybeds and scout for prey. Seeing the animals spend so much time in high places, Rodney Jackson even suggested that *crag leopard* would be a better common name for the animals than *snow leopard*.[6] Since the 1980s, researchers have continued to add to the store of scientific knowledge about snow leopards.

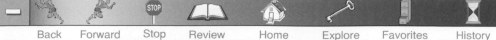

# Chapter 5

# CURRENT STATUS, RESEARCH, AND CONSERVATION EFFORTS

**There** are an estimated 4,000 to 7,000 snow leopards left in the wild. Many small isolated populations are in great danger of local extinction. Snow leopards continue to be threatened by the rapid rise of human population and loss of habitat; increased use of alpine meadows for livestock grazing; reduction in the population of prey species, especially wild goats and sheep; and heavy hunting pressure with the animals' pelts used for clothing and their bones used in Chinese medicine.

## ▶ Thriving in Captivity

While the snow leopard continues to be endangered in the wild, it is thriving in captivity. There are approximately 500 snow leopards in 150 zoos worldwide, with 236 of those in the United States. More snow leopards are found in private collections and on game farms in Europe and North America. Some people have proposed using these captive animals for two purposes: as fur farm animals and as breeding stock to reintroduce to the wild.

▲ *Snow leopards are thriving in captivity, but none now in zoos have yet been reintroduced to the wild.*

## ▶Farmed Leopards

The use of captive snow leopards as fur farm animals is a controversial one. Its proponents say that if put into practice, it could cause the price of snow leopard pelts from the wild to fall so low that those poached illegally would have little value on the world market. This would discourage poachers from taking more animals in the wild. As recently as 1999, coats made from wild snow leopard skins were being sold openly (and illegally) in Kathmandu, Nepal, for $5,500 each. Each coat consisted of four snow leopard skins. The creation of snow leopard fur farms could end this demand for wild snow leopard pelts. But those opposed to this idea point to similar farms in China for captive bears. Rather than decreasing demand for bear parts, they have actually increased it.

## ▶Captive Breeding

The idea of breeding snow leopards in captivity to return them to the wild has been considered by zoos around the world, but no one has yet set up such a program. Captive breeding is not as easy as it might sound. For it to work, the animals must usually be bred in isolation from humans so they do not lose their wildness. They must learn to hunt and act just like their relatives in the wild. Even if they can accomplish this, there is no guarantee that the captive animals will survive once released on their own into the wild. There first must be enough protected habitat for that to happen, and other snow leopards will compete with the reintroduced ones whenever a new cat is released.

## ▶ Snow Leopard SSP

Many zoos are participants in the Snow Leopard Species Survival Plan (SSP), part of a coordinated breeding program among zoos. The goal of the Snow Leopard SSP is to maintain a genetically sound population of snow leopards so that the animals or their offspring may someday be released

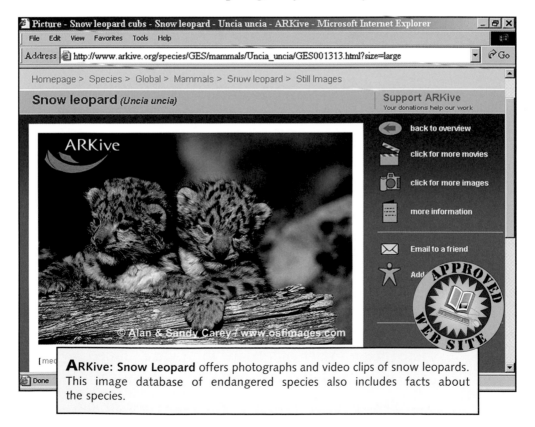

**A**RKive: Snow Leopard offers photographs and video clips of snow leopards. This image database of endangered species also includes facts about the species.

into the wild. When the American Zoo and Aquarium Association introduced the Snow Leopard Species Survival Plan in 1984, its goal was to maintain a population of 250 to 300 animals in more than seventy managed locations in North America. The plan recommended that an average of twenty-five cubs be born each year to maintain a stable population.[1] Recently, the program saw an exciting breakthrough: "As part of a zoo-based research program, the first snow leopard cub ever conceived by artificial insemination has moved the SSP closer to genome banking."[2] That refers to the collection and storage of snow leopard eggs and sperm for future fertilization and reproduction.

If snow leopards go extinct in the wild, scientists still hope to regrow the species through what are called "frozen zoos." In a frozen zoo, embryos and semen of an endangered animal are frozen and preserved indefinitely. Should the species go extinct, this frozen material could theoretically be thawed and used to create new members of the species, which could repopulate wild habitat.

## ▶ Up Close and Personal

You can see some of the animals involved in the Snow Leopard Species Survival Plan by visiting some major American zoos. In August 2006, a snow leopard on loan from Pakistan arrived at New York's Bronx Zoo. In 2005, Leo, a seven-week-old

File   Edit   View   Favorites   Tools   Help

Address  http://www.state.gov/r/pa/ei/pix/b/sat/70080.htm

## Photos: International Cooperation Saves Snow Leopard

**Pakistan, August 8, 2006:** Through the coordinated efforts of the governments of the United States and Pakistan, an orphaned snow leopard cub, one of the world's most endangered mammals, is being transferred from the Naltar valley in northern Pakistan to a temporary home at the Bronx Zoo. Assistant Secretary of State for Oceans, Environment, and Science Claudia A. McMurray, who played a key role in facilitating the transfer, said this cooperative venture is a symbol of the Government of Pakistan's commitment to conservation. It also demonstrates the breadth of US-Pakistani relations and signals an important victory for wildlife worldwide. Below are pictures of the snow leopard sent from Pakistan before he began his journey, provided courtesy of the World Conservation Union.

Media Note | Remarks by Ambassador Crocker | Embassy Pakistan

The Bronx Zoo became the temporary home of an orphaned snow leopard cub from Pakistan in August 2006 thanks to the cooperative efforts of the United States, Pakistan, and conservation organizations. Read more about Leo, pictured, and those who worked to save him, at **U.S. State Department: International Cooperation Saves Cub**.

orphaned cub, had been rescued by a shepherd in the Naltar Valley. The Pakistanis did not have adequate facilities to care for the orphaned cub, so the World Conservation Union-Pakistan worked with the Pakistani government to send Leo to a foreign zoo as part of a captive-breeding program. According to officials with the U.S. government, "Such programs are meant to promote conservation, biodiversity, and rehabilitation of endangered species around the world. The Bronx Zoo in New York is ideal because it has a snow leopard habitat and is one of the few conservation centers participating in the World Conservation Union Species Survival Plan breeding program for snow leopards."[3] At the ceremony welcoming the big cat to the Bronx, Ryan C. Crocker, the U.S. ambassador to Pakistan, remarked, "The successful transfer of this snow leopard to the Bronx Zoo is an impressive example of trans-continental, public-private collaboration."[4]

You can also see snow leopards in Texas at the Houston Zoo; in Seattle, Washington, at the Woodland Park Zoo; in Missouri at the Saint Louis Zoo; and in Providence, Rhode Island, at the Roger Williams Park Zoo.

## ▶ The Work of the International Snow Leopard Trust

The International Snow Leopard Trust (ISLT), based in Seattle, Washington, has worked on the conservation and habitat preservation of snow leopards since 1981. It is the largest and oldest organization working solely to protect the endangered snow leopard and its Central Asian habitat. The ISLT has programs in five nations: China, India, Kyrgyzstan, Mongolia, and Pakistan.

According to the ISLT's statement on its Web site, "At the Snow Leopard Trust we use a combination of approaches that focus on partnering with communities in snow leopard habitat. . . .

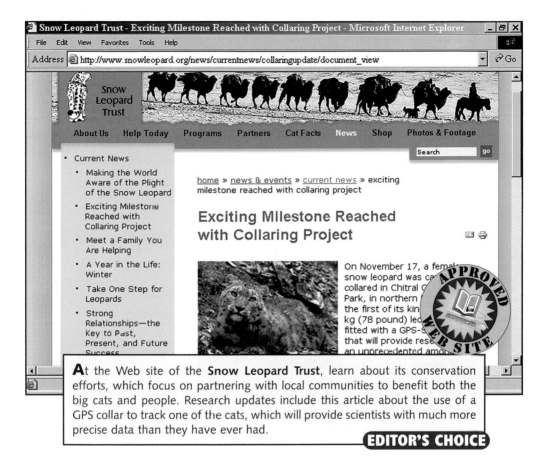

At the Web site of the **Snow Leopard Trust**, learn about its conservation efforts, which focus on partnering with local communities to benefit both the big cats and people. Research updates include this article about the use of a GPS collar to track one of the cats, which will provide scientists with much more precise data than they have ever had.

**EDITOR'S CHOICE**

[A]s we build community partnerships we use science and research to determine key snow leopard habitat, assess wildlife-human conflict levels, and identify potential resources for conservation programs."[5]

The ISLT identifies priority snow leopard habitat through scientific investigation. Then it listens to the people living in communities where snow leopards also live to understand their particular concerns about the cats, working closely with villagers to develop a joint conservation plan.

The Snow Leopard Trust helps local people to establish their own tourist businesses through its Snow Leopard Enterprises program. The people who participate make clothing, folk art, and items for the home such as rugs and embroidered napkins. These handicrafts can also be purchased online from the ISLT Web site.[6] Villagers who have become involved in this commerce no longer rely so heavily on their livestock for their livelihoods. They also start to see the snow leopard in a more favorable light, as an important symbol of their land and as an economically beneficial attraction.

## ▶Helping Communities

The ISLT also helps communities to establish sustainable herding practices. It offers insurance for their domestic livestock against the possibility of attacks by predators including snow leopards. It runs a livestock-vaccination program that protects domestic animals from diseases. The ISLT has also contracted with villagers to agree not to poach snow leopards or hunt bharal, the leopards' prey.

Finally, Snow Leopard Enterprises is involved in education. It holds seminars, prints newsletters, and displays posters about snow leopards in participating villages to increase awareness among the community of the value and benefits of snow leopards.

## ▶ The Work of the Snow Leopard Conservancy

Like the Snow Leopard Trust, the Snow Leopard Conservancy (SLC) is a leader in community-based snow leopard protection programs. The SLC was founded by Rodney Jackson, formerly the ISLT's conservation director.

The SLC focuses on building a strong foundation for conservation within the community so that the protection of snow leopards and their habitat is driven by the people who share that habitat—and have the most to gain or lose by the

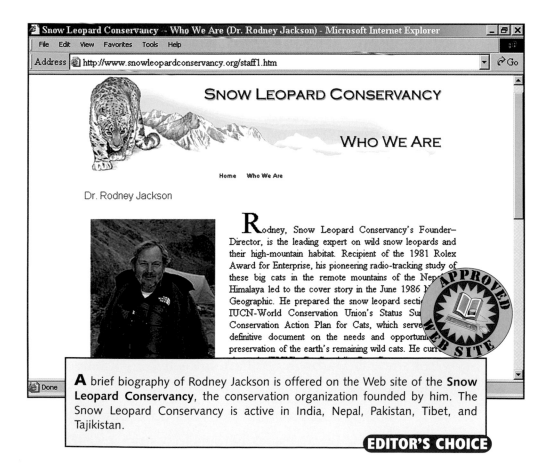

A brief biography of Rodney Jackson is offered on the Web site of the **Snow Leopard Conservancy**, the conservation organization founded by him. The Snow Leopard Conservancy is active in India, Nepal, Pakistan, Tibet, and Tajikistan.

**EDITOR'S CHOICE**

snow leopard's fate. The SLC forms partnerships with organizations in the countries it works in and strives to employ people who understand "local conditions." According to Darla Hillard, who coordinates the SLC's programs and directs small-scale field-based conservation and education activities and education, "Dr. Jackson and his associates mentor these young people, building their expertise and capacity to lead the conservation effort in their own region. This approach leads to community-based stewardship of indigenous wildlife, a transformation of the snow leopard from threat to asset, and the best guarantee that the cats will be protected and conserved for future generations."[7]

## ▶ Community-Based Programs

One of the SLC's most important programs is the design and installation of predator-proof corrals for livestock. This program teaches villagers and herders how to build animal pens using traditional construction techniques that will keep livestock in and snow leopards out. With projects in Nepal, India, and Pakistan, the SLC considers each predator-proof corral to save five snow leopards from retributive killings. Retributive killing is the killing of snow leopards in retaliation for livestock killed by the cats.

Another SLC program helps set up community programs to pay livestock herders to restrict grazing

▲ A herder tends his goats near the Stone Forest in northern China. Conservation programs in some areas of snow leopard habitat have resulted in better livestock pens—and more sympathetic feelings on the part of local communities toward their feline neighbors.

in remote alpine meadows. Such programs help prey species such as blue sheep to thrive, which gives the snow leopards wild animals to eat, rather than feeding on domestic livestock, and contributes to ecotourism, since some tourists want to see blue sheep and wild goats as well as snow leopards.

## Himalayan Homestays

The SLC's award-winning Himalayan Homestays program brings hundreds of ecotourists to indigenous villages in snow leopard territory. The program has many benefits: Local people profit from the tourists who pay them for room and board and for guide services. (With traditional tourism, only outside agencies benefited.) And the tourists benefit by having an authentic experience of life in a Himalayan village. A major travel publication hails the work done by this program as having "single-handedly transformed the common perception of the snow leopard, from that of a dangerous predator that attacks livestock to an animal whose presence draws travelers and provides important economic opportunities."[8]

The SLC has also published a handbook on camera-trapping techniques. Camera trapping is a method by which researchers use remotely triggered cameras set up on trails used by snow leopards. When the cat breaks the infrared beam, it takes its own picture. The photos make it possible to identify individual animals so that population size can be more accurately estimated. It also allows researchers to identify resident animals and track their behaviors over time. The SLC is using this book not only to train other scientists but also for the education of wildlife guards and local villagers. "Knowing the actual leopards that inhabit their neighborhood and being able to monitor their status helps communities become better stewards for the species," says an SLC annual report.[9]

Rodney Jackson has used every means possible to save snow leopards, including appeals through religious leaders. In 2005 he met with the Dalai Lama, the leader of the Tibetan Buddhist faith,

International Society for Endangered Cats Canada: Snow Leopard

The International Society for Endangered Cats (ISEC) Canada is a nonprofit organization dedicated to supporting and promoting wild cat conservation programs. Its Web site offers detailed pages on all species of cats, including the snow leopard.

*Access this Web site from http://www.myreportlinks.com*

and convinced him to support the protection of snow leopards. The Dalai Lama then spoke to thousands of his followers in an appeal: "When you go back to your respective places, remember what I had said and never use, sell, or buy wild animals, their products or derivatives."[10]

The work of the ISLT and the SLC with local communities is creating a new trend of self-sustaining local wildlife stewardship throughout the snow leopard's range, according to Rinchen Wangchuk, Director of SLC-India:

> When we first initiated the Snow Leopard Conservancy, the villagers could not understand why we had chosen for our organization the name of a despised predator. Today, their sentiments are echoed by Tsering Phuntsok of Chilling [a village], "Wild animals are like the ornaments of our mountains!" We know our work is effective, but changing attitudes towards snow leopards will not happen overnight; the [local] communities must see social and economic benefits associated with wildlife protection.[11]

## ▷ Snow Leopard Network

The Snow Leopard Network (SLN) is a global organization that promotes an exchange of ideas among the various conservation groups, governments, and individuals involved in saving the snow leopard. The network grew out of the Snow Leopard Survival Summit held in Seattle, Washington, in 2002, in which experts from around the world gathered to discuss conservation

SNOW LEOPARD NETWORK - Microsoft Internet Explorer

File   Edit   View   Favorites   Tools   Help

Address  http://www.snowleopardnetwork.org/

**SNOW LEOPARD NETWORK HOME**

The Snow Leopard Network is a worldwide organization dedicated to facilitating the exchange of information between individuals around the world for the purpose of snow leopard preservation. Our membership includes leading snow leopard experts in the public, private, and non-profit sectors.

The main goal of this organization is to implement the Snow Leopard Survival Strategy (SLSS), which offers

**SLN News**

Saving a Cat w Precious Pelt

The Seattle Time reports on the st markets of Kabu Afghanistan, and illegal snow leop pelts for sale the
Read more...

Snow Leopard

**The Snow Leopard Network**

The Snow Leopard Network is an international organization that promotes cooperation and an exchange of ideas among groups and individuals involved in snow leopard conservation. Read about the organization's current and ongoing projects at its Web site.

**EDITOR'S CHOICE**

*Access this Web site from http://www.myreportlinks.com*

initiatives. The network's membership has nearly tripled since its founding and continues to expand as more organizations become involved in the effort to save the big cat. Its goals are spelled out in the Snow Leopard Survival Strategy, a plan written by several SLN members, which combines scientific research, conservation actions, and the establishment of government action plans.

## ▶ IUCN-World Conservation Union Cat Specialist Group

Headquartered in Switzerland, the Cat Specialist Group is a network of approximately two hundred cat specialists from around the world who are part of the IUCN-World Conservation Union. This network is responsible for checking the status and the conservation needs of the thirty-six wild cat species living on our planet. The group's work includes updating the Red List status of cats, including the snow leopard.[12]

## ▶ World Wildlife Fund Snow Leopard Program

The World Wildlife Fund (WWF) supports research and habitat conservation projects for the snow leopard in many parts of its range. WWF is also working to put a stop to the illegal traffic in endangered cat pelts and to create and maintain preserves to protect snow leopards and other endangered species.[13]

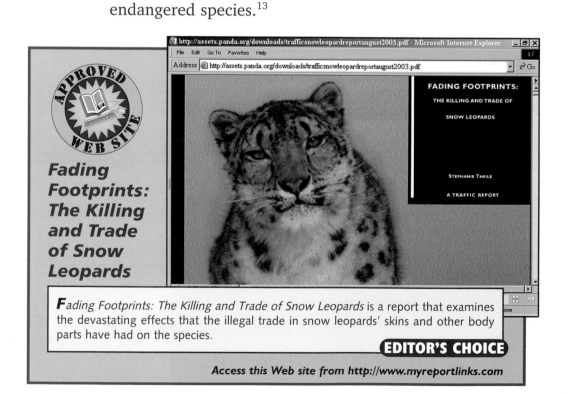

**Fading Footprints: The Killing and Trade of Snow Leopards**

*Fading Footprints: The Killing and Trade of Snow Leopards* is a report that examines the devastating effects that the illegal trade in snow leopards' skins and other body parts have had on the species.

**EDITOR'S CHOICE**

*Access this Web site from http://www.myreportlinks.com*

In Mongolia, WWF created an antipoaching team. It also supports Snow Leopard Enterprises, a nonprofit handicraft enterprise started by the International Snow Leopard Trust. This project offers herders an opportunity to increase their income in return for protecting the snow leopard.

A 2003 study by TRAFFIC (the Trade Records Analysis of Flora and Fauna in Commerce) and the International Snow Leopard Trust found a dramatic decline over the previous decade in the number of big cats in many countries. TRAFFIC is a joint program of the WWF and IUCN, and its agents work to uncover and stop illegal commerce in endangered animals. The 2003 study was the first to assess threats to snow leopards across their entire range. It found that the species was being threatened by illegal killing and trade across Central Asia, Russia, and the Himalayas. The study's population estimate of only 4,000 to 7,000 snow leopards left in the world made the mountain-dwelling big cats as endangered as tigers.[14]

## ▶How You Can Help

One of the easiest ways for you to get involved in saving snow leopards is through an environmental group such as the International Snow Leopard Trust (ISLT), the Snow Leopard Conservancy (SLC), or the World Wildlife Fund (WWF).

WWF - Snow leopards (Uncia uncia) - Microsoft Internet Explorer

File   Edit   View   Favorites   Tools   Help

Address  http://www.panda.org/about_wwf/where_we_work/asia_pacific/where/nepal/our_solutions/thematic_soluti   Go

**Snow Leopards (Uncia uncia)**

Nepal

About WWF          How You Can Help          News & Facts          FAQ          search

Home > About WWF > Where We Work > Asia > Solutions by Country > Nepal > Our Solutions > By theme... > Species > Snow Leopard

Nepal

▸ Our Solutions
  How We Work
  By locations...
  By theme...
    ✦ Forests
    ✦ Species
      ✦ Rhinoceros
      ✦ Tiger
      ✦ Elephant
      ✦ Snow Leopard
      ✦ Gangetic Dolphin
    ✦ Climate Change
    ✦ Freshwater
  Projects
▸ News
▸ Office Information
▸ Profile

**Snow leopards (Uncia uncia)**

**Status and Distribution of Snow Leopard**

Snow leopards (*Uncia uncia*) are found only in the mountains of central Asia and the Himalayas. It is estimated that there are about 4,510-7,350 snow leopards. The total potential snow leopard habitat is about 1,835,000 km 2 in 12 snow leopard range countries. In addition, some 600-700 animals survive in zoos around the

**A**t this World Wildlife Fund site, read about the threats to snow leopards and find out what is being done to protect this endangered cat.

*Access this Web site from http://www.myreportlinks.com*

You can start by going to the ISLT home page and signing up for news about snow leopards that will be sent to you by e-mail.[15] The more you learn about these animals, the more you can do to protect them. You may even want to begin studying to become a wildlife biologist so you, too, like George Schaller or Rodney Jackson, can become a leader in protecting snow leopards and other big cats.

The ISLT site also invites you to "adopt" a snow leopard or a whole snow leopard family. With a contribution, you receive an adoption certificate, a snow leopard toy, a snow leopard fact sheet and photos, and a one-year's membership in the International Snow Leopard Trust. The site also offers products for sale that were made by the people who live in the remote mountains of Central Asia where snow leopards also live.

## ▶ Join a Group

You can also choose to join the Snow Leopard Conservancy. With your family or classmates, organize a fund-raiser and donate the proceeds to the SLC. Or you might want to purchase snow leopard photographs or prints from the SLC that you can use in your own classroom talks about snow leopards.

You can also adopt a snow leopard with the SLC. Every adoption packet includes a portrait taken by a camera trap of a wild snow leopard that your contribution is supporting, an official snow leopard adoption certificate, a snow leopard fact sheet and frequently asked questions, an overview of the SLC's programs, and photographs and biographies of SLC staff. The SLC Web site offers snow leopard books and posters for sale as well, with the monies going toward conservation of the big cats.[16]

The World Wildlife Fund has its own snow leopard protection program. Find out more about it at the WWF Web site. You can make donations, adopt a snow leopard, give a gift membership, or buy from their online shop.[17] The WWF also supports legislation that helps to protect the world's big cats and other wildlife.

## ▶Even More You Can Do

Your efforts to save snow leopards begin, however, by learning as much as you can about them. By learning about their life cycle, about their value to people and to the world's mountains, and about what threatens them, you can become a snow leopard ambassador. You can teach others about this endangered species. You are doing that right now by reading this book and by learning more from the Web sites it recommends.

You can educate your family, friends, and classmates and get them to team up with you to spring into action to conduct e-mail and snail mail letter-writing campaigns to United Nations and

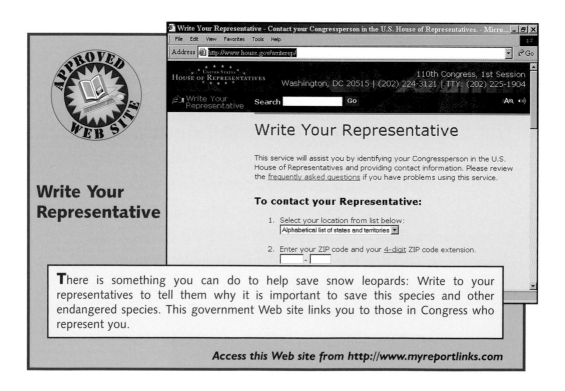

**Write Your Representative**

There is something you can do to help save snow leopards: Write to your representatives to tell them why it is important to save this species and other endangered species. This government Web site links you to those in Congress who represent you.

*Access this Web site from http://www.myreportlinks.com*

United States government officials who can help snow leopards by making laws or putting together treaties. If you are a student and care about the future of snow leopards, you could consider a career in conservation biology.

There may be fewer than seven thousand snow leopards left in the world, and even that small estimate might be too high. Considering all the dangers these beautiful big cats face every day, they need all the help we can give them.

# Chapter 6

# CHANCES FOR SURVIVAL AND RECOVERY

**The** International Snow Leopard Trust, the Snow Leopard Conservancy, the World Wildlife Fund, and other conservation groups and individuals have spearheaded the fight to save snow leopards. Unfortunately, they work with relatively small budgets and can only run projects in a few communities throughout the snow leopard's vast range. Among the things that still need to be done are the creation of more community development projects like those undertaken by the ISLT and SLC for local wildlife stewardship. These programs need to be widespread and supported by international and national government agencies.

If snow leopards are to be protected, the wildlife protection laws of the twelve countries in which snow leopards live need to be more strictly enforced. Since many of these countries are poor and lack the funding they would need to do this, the United Nations could offer legal advice and assistance to them. The fines, jail time, and other penalties for breaking these laws also need to be increased. The snow leopard home range states should also consider instituting "whistle blower" policies where those who report the illegal killing, possession, or trade of a snow leopard are rewarded for their environmental stewardship. It would also help if Kyrgyzstan and Tajikistan were to join CITES.

It is also important that law enforcement be improved. Home range nations need to better patrol known snow leopard trade routes, wildlife markets, fur shops, tourist shops, and important border crossings. National governments also need to establish antipoaching police teams to focus exclusively on the illegal hunting and trading of snow leopards. Conservation education must be

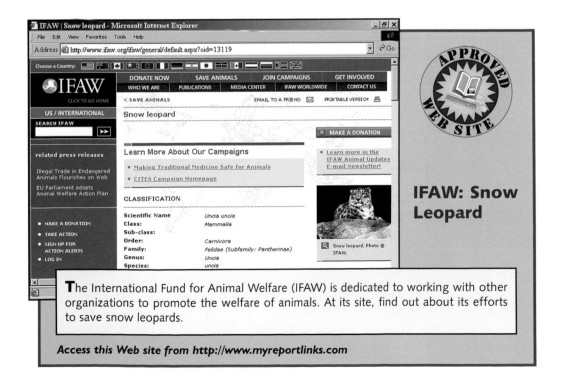

**IFAW: Snow Leopard**

The International Fund for Animal Welfare (IFAW) is dedicated to working with other organizations to promote the welfare of animals. At its site, find out about its efforts to save snow leopards.

*Access this Web site from http://www.myreportlinks.com*

People pose the greatest threat to snow leopards. If these beautiful cats are to survive, people will have to decide it is worth saving them.

improved, and local people need to be given significant incentives to stop poaching and hunting snow leopards.

A publicity campaign could be started in China and other countries to raise awareness of how snow leopards and their mountain ecosystems can be conserved by the people themselves who live within the snow leopard's range. Educational posters, booklets, and radio and television programs should be produced in local languages and widely distributed.

**Snow Leopards**

**Common Name:** Snow Leopard
**Kingdom:** Animalia
**Phylum:** Chordata (Vertebrata)
**Class:** Mammalia
**Order:** Carnivora
**Family:** Felidae
**Genus:** Pantherinae Uncia
**Species:** uncia

Conservation organizations closer to home are also trying to save snow leopards. Big Cat Rescue is a nonprofit organization in Florida whose focus is educating the public on the rescue and conservation of these animals. The **Big Cat Rescue: Snow Leopards** page offers links to information on current legislation involving big cats.

Conservationists could try instead to make the manufacturers, sellers, and consumers of traditional Chinese medicines more aware of the damage that snow leopard poaching is doing to the species' wild populations.

People throughout Asia and the rest of the world can do something meaningful to save snow leopards now. We all need to learn more about the big cats' plight and their importance to mountain ecosystems. Saving the snow leopard will take more than caging a few zoo specimens. It requires the preservation and restoration of habitat and of other animals throughout Central Asia. It is a big job, demanding the commitment and cooperation of many peoples and nations.

## The Key to Saving Snow Leopards

But no matter how much is done worldwide, it is ultimately the people living in the lands where snow leopards also live who will determine the big cats' fate. If livestock herding practices can continue to be improved, snow leopards will kill fewer domestic animals. Herds will need to be attended and well guarded by experienced adult herders or by trained herding dogs. Predator-proof corrals must continue to be built for domestic livestock throughout the snow leopard's home range. By using improved grazing methods, herders and farmers can save the wild grasses that support wild sheep and goats, which will also save the snow leopards that feed on those wild animals.

Governments need to be pressured to offer communities economic incentives to conserve snow leopards. This means more locally based ecotourism, more locally trained wildlife guides and rangers, and more conservation officers from the countries involved. Home range countries also need to put in place insurance programs covering domestic livestock to protect people against unexpected snow leopard attacks on their herds.

## Caring for People and Snow Leopards

When asked how many snow leopards remain in the wild, Rodney Jackson raised another, more important, question:

> A deeper, more serious question faces the conservationist: What is to be done about the increasing number of hardy mountain people who are going to bed with hungry bellies? How can we possibly expect a Bhote [native] in Dolphu, a Chitrali [native] in Pakistan, or a Golok [native] in Qinghai to care about snow leopards and blue sheep if they or their children are swamped by poverty and want? Unless we can find ways of improving their standard of living, wildlife conservation faces a dismal future. Conservation must be better integrated with development.[1]

He insists that the only way snow leopards will survive is if local people see a reason to protect them. One promising local industry in many parts

▲ A future in which snow leopards like this one still roam the mountains of Central Asia is a future we can make happen.

of the cats' range is ecotourism. If people can make more money by showing tourists the snow leopard and its habitat, then they will be less likely to hunt and kill the animals. As Rodney Jackson points out, "[P]eople are a fact of life within nearly all Himalayan national parks. The survival of wildlife and their habitat depends upon the goodwill and aspirations of the local people. The sooner we embrace them in the solution, the better."[2] If snow leopards are to survive as a species, the people who live among them need to survive—and thrive—as well.

*In 1973, Congress took the farsighted step of creating the Endangered Species Act, widely regarded as the world's strongest and most effective wildlife conservation law. It set an ambitious goal: to reverse the alarming trend of human-caused extinction that threatened the ecosystems we all share.*

Each book in this series explores the life of an endangered animal. The books tell how and why the animals have become endangered and explain the efforts being made to restore their populations.

The United States Fish and Wildlife Service and the National Marine Fisheries Service share responsibility for administration of the Endangered Species Act. Over time, animals are added to, reclassified in, or removed from the federal list of Endangered and Threatened Wildlife and Plants. At the time of publication, all the animals in this series were listed as endangered species. The most up-to-date list can be found at **http://www.fws.gov/endangered/wildlife.html**.

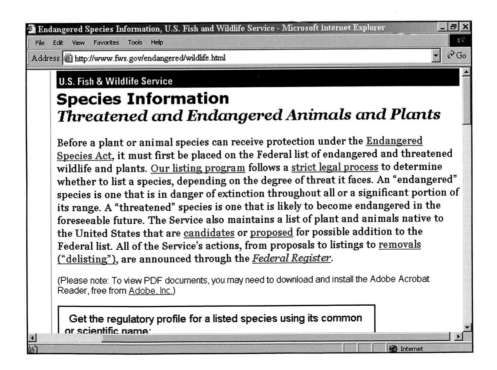

## Report Links

**The Internet sites described below can be accessed at**
**http://www.myreportlinks.com**

▶**Snow Leopard Conservancy**
**\*\*Editor's Choice\*\*** The group's site offers a window to its work saving the big cats of Central Asia.

▶**Snow Leopard Trust**
**\*\*Editor's Choice\*\*** This organization is saving snow leopards and the people who share their habitat.

▶**The Snow Leopard Network**
**\*\*Editor's Choice\*\*** This international organization promotes an exchange of conservation ideas.

▶*Fading Footprints: The Killing and Trade of Snow Leopards*
**\*\*Editor's Choice\*\*** Read an in-depth report on the illegal trade in endangered snow leopards.

▶**NATURE:** *Silent Roar: Searching for the Snow Leopard*
**\*\*Editor's Choice\*\*** At this PBS site, find out about conservationists' search for the elusive snow leopard.

▶**Woodland Park Zoo: Snow Leopard**
**\*\*Editor's Choice\*\*** Visit the Woodland Park zoo to see its snow leopard.

▶**Animal Diversity Web:** *Uncia uncia*
A fact sheet on snow leopards and photos of the cats are offered by this university site.

▶**ARKive: Snow Leopard**
An online database features images of endangered animals around the world, including the snow leopard.

▶**BBC News: "Snow Leopard Diary"**
A BBC News article documents a groundbreaking snow leopard research project in Pakistan.

▶**Big Cat Rescue: Snow Leopards**
A nonprofit organization's efforts to save big cats through education is profiled.

▶**The Big Cats—Snow Leopard**
A photo gallery of snow leopard images and facts about the species are offered.

▶**Central Asia: Villagers Encouraged to Protect Snow Leopards**
Radio Free Europe's site offers this article on the threats to Kyrgyzstan's few remaining snow leopards.

▶**CNN.com: Snow Leopards Spotted on Top of World**
In 2004, snow leopards were found on the slopes of Mount Everest for the first time in many years.

▶**IFAW: Snow Leopard**
Find out about the International Fund for Animal Welfare's efforts to preserve snow leopards.

▶**International Society for Endangered Cats Canada: Snow Leopard**
This Canadian Web site offers information on all cat species.

## Report Links

# The Internet sites described below can be accessed at http://www.myreportlinks.com

▶ **The IUCN Red List of Threatened Species: *Uncia uncia***
Read about the threats to snow leopards listed by an international organization.

▶ **The Megafauna Man: George Schaller**
The fifty-year career of biologist George Schaller is celebrated on this *National Geographic* site.

▶ ***National Geographic Adventure*: Searching for Snow Leopards**
Join a National Geographic team as they go in search of snow leopards in Ladakh, India.

▶ **NPR: "Protecting the Snow Leopard From Poachers"**
A National Public Radio correspondent learns about snow leopard conservation in Mongolia.

▶ **Philadelphia Zoo: Snow Leopards**
The Philadelphia Zoo's Big Cat Falls welcomes snow leopards.

▶ ***The Seattle Times*: Saving a Cat With a Precious Pelt**
A newspaper article looks at the illegal trade in snow leopard pelts in Afghanistan.

▶ **Snow Leopard**
A Defenders of Wildlife page offers information on snow leopards.

▶ **Snow Leopards (*Uncia uncia*)**
At this WWF site, read about the organization's work saving snow leopards.

▶ **TRAFFIC**
Find out more about the illegal trade in wildlife from this organization dedicated to stopping it.

▶ **USFWS Endangered Species Program Kid's Corner**
This USFWS Web site offers ways you can help save endangered species.

▶ **U.S. State Department: International Cooperation Saves Cub**
An orphaned cub finds a welcome at the Bronx Zoo.

▶ **Wildlife Conservation Network: Conservation Fellows**
This Web site offers information about Rodney Jackson.

▶ **Wildlife Conservation Society: Kyrgyzstan: Snow Leopard Conservation**
Learn about snow leopard conservation in the Tien Shans.

▶ **World Wildlife Fund: Snow Leopards**
Read about the work of the World Wildlife Fund in saving snow leopards.

▶ **Write Your Representative**
Find links to your congressional representatives on this government site.

**advocate**—One in favor of, or who supports, something, such as a cause.

**captive breeding**—The breeding of species in zoos with the intention of someday returning offspring to the wild. Snow leopards are no longer removed from the wild, but those already in zoos are breeding well there.

**carnivore**—A meat-eating animal.

**charismatic megaspecies (or megafauna)**—Big animals that are few in number and on the brink of extinction that attract a huge amount of public sympathy, attention, and support for preservation. Snow leopards, tigers, and whales are examples.

**crepuscular**—Describes animals that are most active around dawn and dusk.

**critical habitat**—Under the Endangered Species Act, the entire functioning ecosystem in which an endangered animal lives.

**degraded**—Impaired or worn down; made less valuable or useful.

**ecotourism**—Tourism that focuses on wildlife and the natural places in which animals live without harming those animals or lands.

**gestation**—The time involved in a pregnancy until a newborn arrives.

**home range**—The territory that a species or subspecies inhabits.

**poaching**—Illegal hunting of an animal or plant.

**predator**—An animal that lives by eating another.

**prey**—An animal taken by a predator as food.

**rabid**—Afflicted with rabies, an acute viral disease that is often fatal.

**Red List**—A list compiled by the IUCN-World Conservation Union of animals and plants that are threatened worldwide.

**retractable**—Able to be drawn back or in, as cats' claws.

**retributive killing**—The revengeful killing of a species. Snow leopards are killed by farmers when the big cats break into livestock pens to feed on domestic animals.

**rosette**—An irregular rose-shaped marking of varying size, usually dark brown or black, found on many wild cat species, including snow leopards.

**scree**—Loose rock debris at the base of a cliff or steep incline.

**sexual maturity**—The age at which an animal is able to mate for the first time.

**subspecies**—A population of a species that has evolved different physical and genetic characteristics from the rest of the species.

**taxidermist**—A person who prepares and stuffs animal heads and skins for mounting.

## Chapter 1. Tracking—and Saving— an Elusive Cat

1. George B. Schaller, *Stones of Silence: Journeys in the Himalaya* (New York: Viking Press, 1979), pp. 8–9.

2. Rodney Jackson, *Snow Leopard Conservancy*, "Field Notes by Rodney Jackson, Leh, Ladakh, February 18, 2005," <http://www.snowleopardconservancy.org/pdf/RodFieldNotesFeb05.pdf> (February 1, 2007).

3. Philadelphiazoo.org, "Bank of America Big Cat Falls at the Philadelphia Zoo," n.d., <http://www.philadelphiazoo.org/index.php?id=2_2_5> (August 14, 2006).

4. Ibid.

5. *Chattanoogan.com*, "New Snow Leopard Exhibit to Open at Chattanooga Zoo," August 10, 2006, <http://www.chattanoogan.com/articles/article_90780.asp> (August 14, 2006).

6. Darla Hillard, *Vanishing Tracks: Four Years Among the Snow Leopards of Nepal* (New York: William Morrow, 1989), p. 317.

7. Ibid., pp. 317–318.

8. Ibid., p. 318

## Chapter 2. All About Snow Leopards

1. Datasegment.com Online Dictionary, *felis uncia*, n.d., <http://onlinedictionary.datasegment.com/word/felis+uncia> (June 27, 2006).

2. Big Cats Online, "Snow Leopard, *Uncia uncia*," n.d., <http://www.dialspace.dial.pipex.com/agarman/snowlep.htm> (June 27, 2006).

3. Zoo.org, "Animal Fact Sheets: Snow Leopard," n.d., <http://www.zoo.org/educate/fact_sheets/snow_leopard/sleopard.htm> (August 14, 2006).

4. S. Bagchi and C. Mishra, "Living with large carnivores: predation on livestock by the snow leopard (*Uncia uncia*)," *Journal of Zoology*, the Zoological Society of London, vol. 268, 2006, pp. 217, 222.

5. George B. Schaller, *Stones of Silence: Journeys in the Himalaya* (New York: Viking Press, 1979), pp. 24–25.

6. Erwin A. Bauer, *The Last Big Cats: An Untamed Spirit* (Stillwater, Minn.: Voyageur Press, 2003), p. 107.

7. Garma Chang, "The Song of the Snow Range," from *The Hundred Thousand Songs of Milarepa* (New York: Harper & Row, 1962), cited on Snow Leopard Conservancy: Myths and Legends, "Tibetan Myths Surrounding Snow Leopards," n.d., <http://www.snowleopardconservancy.org/tibmyths.htm> (June 27, 2006).

8. Dr. John Mock, *Snow Leopards, Mountain Spirits, and Sacred Space in Northern Pakistan*, Snow Leopard Conservancy: Myths and Legends, 2004, <http://www.snowleopardconservancy.org/pakmyths.htm> (June 27, 2006).

9. Som. B. Ale and Bhaskar S. Karky, *Observations on Conservation of Snow Leopards in Nepal*, Snow Leopard Conservancy: Myths and Legends, "Nepalese Myths Surrounding Snow Leopards," n.d., <http://www.snowleopardconservancy.org/nepmyths.htm> (June 27, 2006).

## Chapter 3. Threats to the Species

1. The International Institute of Applied Systems Analysis, "World Population: Major Trends," n.d., <http://www.iiasa.ac.at/Research/LUC/Papers/gkh1/chap1.htm#high_5> (June 27, 2006).

2. Erwin A. Bauer, *The Last Big Cats: An Untamed Spirit* (Stillwater, Minn.: Voyageur Press, 2003), pp. 108–109.

3. Darla Hillard, *The Snow Leopard Conservancy*, comments as advisor to this book.

4. Bauer, p. 109.

5. World Wildlife Fund, FOCUS Newsletter, "Snow Leopards in Decline," 2003.

6. Stephanie Thiele, *Fading Footsteps: The Killing and Trade of Snow Leopards*. TRAFFIC International, August 2003, <http://www.traffic.org/content/218.pdf> (January 21, 2007).

7. *OneWorld South Asia*, Sanjaya Dhakal, "Nepal's Vanishing Snow Leopards," May 11, 2004, <http://southasia.oneworld.net/article/view/85804/1/42> (June 27, 2006).

## Chapter 4. Protecting the Snow Leopard

1. *Convention on International Trade in Endangered Species of Wild Fauna and Flora*, "What is CITES?" n.d., <http://www.cites.org/eng/disc/what.shtml> (June 27, 2006).

2. *Convention on Migratory Species*, "Introduction to the Convention on Migratory Species," n.d., <http://www.cms.int/about/intro.htm> (June 27, 2006).

3. Erwin A. Bauer, *The Last Big Cats: An Untamed Spirit* (Stillwater, Minn.: Voyageur Press, 2003), p. 106.

4. Jan-Olov Andersson et al., "Is the Snow Leopard (*Uncia uncia*) Endangered?" Seventh International Symposium on High Mountain Remote Sensing Cartography, International Cartographic Association, 2002, p. 22.

5. Bauer, p. 107.

6. Ibid.

## Chapter 5. Current Status, Research, and Conservation Efforts

1. *Como Park Zoo & Conservatory*, St. Paul, Minnesota, "Snow Leopard *Uncia uncia*," n.d., <http://www.comozooconservatory.org/zoo/snowleopard.html> (August 14, 2006).

2. Ibid.

3. USINFO.STATE.GOV, Cecelia Martin, "Bronx Zoo Provides New Home for Pakistani Snow Leopard,"

August 8, 2006, <http://usinfo.state.gov/xarchives/display. html?p=washfile-english&y=2006&m=August&x= 200608081806162scnitram7.682437e-02> (January 29, 2007).

4. Ibid.

5. *International Snow Leopard Trust*, "Our Conservation Philosophy," n.d., <http://www .snowleopard.org/about/philosophy> (June 27, 2006).

6. Ibid., "Shop," n.d. <http://www.snowleopard.org/ shop/> (June 27, 2006).

7. Darla Hillard, *The Snow Leopard Conservancy*, comments as advisor to this book.

8. *Snow Leopard Conservancy Annual Report 2005*, "Conservation Highlights," p. 4.

9. *Snow Leopard Conservancy Annual Report 2005*, "How Do Camera Traps Save Snow Leopards?" p. 2.

10. *Snow Leopard Conservancy Annual Report 2005*, Rodney Jackson, "Building Community Capacity for Saving Snow Leopards," p. 1.

11. *Snow Leopard Conservancy Annual Report 2004*, "Transforming Conflict to Coexistence," p. 1.

12. *IUCN/SSC Cat Specialist Group*, "Welcome to the Portal of the IUCN/SSC Cat Specialist Group," n.d., <http://www.catsg.org/> (June 27, 2006).

13. *World Wildlife Fund*, "Snow Leopards," n.d., <http://www.worldwildlife.org/snowleopards/> (June 27, 2006).

14. Stephanie Thiele, *Fading Footsteps: The Killing and Trade of Snow Leopards*, TRAFFIC International, August 2003, <http://www.traffic.org/content/218 .pdf> (January 21, 2007).

15. *International Snow Leopard Trust*, "Where Conservation Starts with Communities," n.d., <http://www.snowleopard.org/> (June 27, 2006).

16. *Snow Leopard Conservancy*, "Home Page," n.d., <http://www.snowleopardconservancy.org/> (June 27, 2006).

17. *World Wildlife Fund*, "Snow Leopards," n.d., <http://www.worldwildlife.org/snowleopards/> (June 27, 2006).

## Chapter 6. Chances for Survival and Recovery

1. Darla Hillard, *Vanishing Tracks: Four Years Among the Snow Leopards of Nepal* (New York: William Morrow, 1989), p. 315.

2. Ibid., p. 316.

Aaseng, Nathan. *Wild Shots: The World of the Wildlife Photographer*. Brookfield, Conn.: Millbrook Press, 2001.

Currie, Stephen. *The Himalayas*. Detroit: Thomson Gale, 2004.

Dyer, Hadley, and Bobbie Kalman. *Endangered Leopards*. New York: Crabtree Publishers, 2005.

Gamble, Cyndi. *Leopards: Natural History and Conservation*. Stillwater, Minn.: Voyageur Press, 2004.

Greenberg, Daniel A. *Leopards*. New York: Benchmark Books, 2002.

Jackson, Donna M. *The Wildlife Detectives: How Forensic Scientists Fight Crimes Against Nature*. Boston: Houghton Mifflin Company, 2000.

Kalman, Bobbie. *India: The Land*. New York: Crabtree Publishers, 2001.

Kazem, Halima. *Afghanistan*. Milwaukee: Gareth Stevens Publishers, 2003.

Klevansky, Rhonda. *Big Cats*. London: Anness Publishing, Ltd., 2000.

Matthiessen, Peter. *The Snow Leopard*. New York: Penguin, 1987.

Patent, Dorothy Hinshaw. *Big Cats*. New York: Walker & Co., 2005.

Thomas, Peggy. *Big Cat Conservation*. Brookfield, Conn.: Twenty-first Century Books, 2000.